Option
Volatility
&
Pricing
Workbook

Option Volatility

&

Pricing Workbook

PRACTICING ADVANCED TRADING STRATEGIES AND TECHNIQUES

SHELDON NATENBERG

New York Chicago San Francisco Athens London Madrid
Mexico City Milan New Delhi Singapore Sydney Toronto

8 9 10 11 12   CD   27 26 25 24 23

ISBN   978-1-260-11693-9
MHID   1-260-11693-X

e-ISBN   978-1-260-11694-6
e-MHID   1-260-11694-8

This publication is designed to provide accurate and authoritative information in regard to the subject matter covered. It is sold with the understanding that neither the author nor the publisher is engaged in rendering legal, accounting, securities trading, or other professional services. If legal advice or other expert assistance is required, the services of a competent professional person should be sought.
>   *—From a Declaration of Principles jointly adopted by a Committee of the*
>   *American Bar Association and a Committee of Publishers*

McGraw-Hill Education books are available at special quantity discounts to use as premiums and sales promotions or for use in corporate training programs. To contact a representative, please visit the Contact Us pages at www.mhprofessional.com.

Contents

Introduction

Successful option trading can be difficult. Of that there can be no doubt. It does not take long for a new trader to realize that a "surefire" strategy is just a quick way to lose money. Moreover, the complexities of the option market often cause a prospective trader to become discouraged and simply give up in frustration.

This does not mean that success in option trading is an unattainable goal. But in order to reach that goal it is necessary to gain a full understanding of options, including the principles of option evaluation, strategy selection, risk management, and market dynamics. While this knowledge can be gained through actual trading experience, for a new trader with no foundation, mastering these principles simply by trading can be an extended, and perhaps costly, undertaking.

So where should a new trader begin? A good place to start is with a well-written text on options, of which there are many. It is important for a new trader to find a book with which he or she is comfortable. Some texts take a theoretical approach to options, with the expectation that the reader will have a solid grasp of advanced mathematics. Others take a more intuitive approach, but are still able to cover the most important aspects of option trading. Additionally, universities, exchanges, and brokerage firms may offer classes on options that are open to the public and can be a valuable tool in the educational process. Firms that trade options professionally—financial institutions, hedge funds, market-making firms—often have internal education programs to train their traders. These, unfortunately, are rarely open to the public.

Once a trader has the necessary foundation, the next step is to practice and become comfortable with what has been learned. This is the goal of this workbook. By completing the exercises contained herein a trader will achieve a working understanding of the important principles, as well as a comfort level that will enable him or her to enter the option market with increased confidence.

Finally, the aspiring trader must actually enter the option marketplace and apply in the real world what has been learned. While success can never be guaranteed, the efforts that have been made mastering the principles of option evaluation and risk management will give the trader the best chance of reaching his or her goal.

The exercises in this book cover a broad range of topics, from the very basic to quite advanced. A professional trader who needs a complete understanding of options should plan to complete all the exercises. Those with a specialized option application in mind—hedgers, speculators, portfolio managers—may find some exercises more valuable than others. And indeed, it may be reasonable to skip over some of the more advanced exercises.

Although this workbook was initially intended to accompany my book *Option Volatility and Pricing*, for most readers the workbook can probably stand alone. Many of the exercises are preceded with a brief discussion of the principles involved, and the answers and explanations to each exercise should be reasonably clear. Moreover, in the hands of a capable instructor, the exercises can form the basis for a complete course in option trading. The exercises can also be used as templates for additional exercises on the same topic.

For those exercises requiring computation, depending on whether the calculations are done by hand, with the aid of a calculator, or on a spreadsheet, there may be some rounding errors resulting in answers slightly different from those given in the in the answer section. However, these errors should be very small. Whether the answers are correct or not should be obvious.

Every effort has been made to avoid exercises and questions that are ambiguous or have multiple solutions. This is obviously necessary in a workbook of this type. Unfortunately in the real world of option trading there may not be one correct and unambiguous solution to every trading situation.

Option
Volatility
&
Pricing
Workbook

CHAPTER 1

Contract Settlement and Cash Flow

1. **Stock-type settlement.** In stock-type settlement the buyer must immediately pay the seller the full value of the contract, and all profits and losses are unrealized until the position is closed out.

   a. Ignoring interest considerations, describe the cash flow, realized and unrealized profit or loss, and the cumulative profit or loss resulting from the following series of trades in a stock. For purposes of realized profit or loss, the oldest trade is the basis for each calculation.

TRADE SEQUENCE	STOCK PRICE	TRADE	OPEN SHARE POSITION	CASH FLOW CREDIT (+) OR DEBIT (−)	CUMULATIVE CASH CREDIT (+) OR DEBIT (−)	CUMULATIVE PROFIT (+) OR LOSS (−)		TOTAL CUMULATIVE PROFIT (+) OR LOSS (−)
						REALIZED	UNREALIZED	
1 (initial trade)	$46.78	buy 3,000 shares						
2	$45.91	buy 1,000 shares						
3	$47.63	sell 1,200 shares						
4	$46.15	buy 500 shares						
5	$49.20	sell 1,100 shares						
6	$48.55	sell 700 shares						
7	$48.08	sell 1,500 shares						

b. Assume that annual interest rates are 6.00% and that all trades were made at one-month intervals, where one month is exactly 1/12 of a year. What is the interest credit or debit at the end of each one-month period?

PERIOD	CASH POSITION AT BEGINNING OF PERIOD	INTEREST CREDIT (+) OR DEBIT (–) OVER THE PERIOD
1		
2		
3		
4		
5		
6		

c. Ignoring interest compounding (interest on the interest), what is the total interest credit or debit over the entire trade sequence?

d. Including the interest credit or debit, what is the total profit or loss resulting from the entire series of trades?

2. **Futures-type settlement.** In futures-type settlement no cash changes hands between the buyer and seller when a trade is initially made. However, both parties must deposit the required margin with the exchange or clearing house. As the futures price rises or falls, there is a variation credit or debit equal to the amount of the futures price change, and all profits and losses are immediately realized.

A futures contract is currently trading at 625.80 with a point value of $200 (1.00 = $200). The margin requirement is $5,000 per contract.

a. What is the notional value of the futures contract?

b. Ignoring interest considerations, describe the cash flow, realized and unrealized profit or loss, and the cumulative profit or loss resulting from the following series of futures trades.

TRADE SEQUENCE	FUTURES PRICE	TRADE	OPEN FUTURES POSITION	MARGIN REQUIREMENT	CASH FLOW (VARIATION) CREDIT (+) OR DEBIT (−)	CUMULATIVE PROFIT (+) OR LOSS (−)		TOTAL CUMULATIVE PROFIT (+) OR LOSS (−)
						REALIZED	UNREALIZED	
1	625.80	sell 25						
2	621.60	buy 5						
3	633.00	sell 10						
4	617.50	no trade						
5	608.90	buy 20						
6	612.00	sell 5						
7	619.50	buy 15						

c. In theory, interest can be earned on a margin deposit, so there will be no interest gain or loss on a margin deposit. The cost of borrowing the required margin will be offset by the interest earned on the margin. However, as the price of the futures contract rises or falls, there will be an interest gain or loss on any variation credit or debit.

Suppose that annual interest rates are 7.80% and that all trades are made at one-week intervals, where one week is exactly 1/52 of a year. What is the interest credit or debit resulting from the variation cash flow at the end of each weekly period?

PERIOD	VARIATION CASH AT BEGINNING OF PERIOD	INTEREST CREDIT(+) OR DEBIT(−) ON VARIATION OVER THE NEXT PERIOD
1		
2		
3		
4		
5		
6		

d. Ignoring interest compounding (interest on the interest), what is the total interest credit or debit over the entire trade sequence?

total variation interest:	total margin interest:	total interest:

e. Including the interest credit or debit, what is the total profit or loss resulting from the entire series of trades?

CHAPTER 2

Forward Pricing

1. If S is the current stock price, t is the time to maturity, r is an annual interest rate, and D are the expected dividends prior to maturity, then using simple interest, and ignoring interest on dividends, the forward price F for a stock can be approximated as:

$$F = S \times (1 + r \times t) - D$$

Using this relationship, what are the following forward prices? For purposes of this exercise assume that a year is made up of 365 days, 52 weeks, or 12 months.

	STOCK PRICE	TIME TO MATURITY	EXPECTED DIVIDENDS	INTEREST RATE	FORWARD PRICE
a.	46.85	2 months	0	4.80%	
b.	94.66	10 weeks	.50	2.75%	
c.	53.28	216 days	.30	6.10%	
d.	130.00	4 weeks	.75	3.22%	
e.	19.70	5 months	.16	8.31%	

2. A stock that is currently trading at 123.15 is expected to pay a semiannual dividend of 2.60, with the next dividend payment occurring in two months. Including interest earned on dividends, if annual interest rates are 5.30%, what is a one-year forward price for the stock? (Assume that the same interest of 5.30% applies to all cash flows.)

3. A futures contract can be thought of as an exchange-traded forward contract. Using simple interest, and ignoring interest on dividends, calculate the following stock prices. For purposes of this exercise assume that a year is made up of 365 days, 52 weeks, or 12 months.

	FUTURES PRICE	TIME TO MATURITY	EXPECTED DIVIDENDS	INTEREST RATE	STOCK PRICE
a.	39.95	3 months	.10	3.75%	
b.	114.10	19 weeks	.62	7.11%	
c.	80.76	35 days	.25	5.00%	

4. A stock forward contract with 84 days to maturity is trading at 76.95.

    a. Ignoring interest on dividends, if the underlying stock is trading at 76.60 and interest rates are 4.25%, what is the implied dividend?

    b. The same stock forward contract with 84 days to maturity is trading at 77.30. If the underlying stock is trading at 76.70 and a dividend of .51 is expected over the life of the forward contract, what is the implied interest rate?

5. If C is the current price of a commodity, t is the time to maturity, r is an annual interest rate, and s is storage and insurance costs to maturity, then using simple interest, the forward price F for a physical commodity can be approximated as:

$$F = C \times (1 + r \times t) + s$$

a. A physical commodity is currently trading at a cash price of 463.25 per unit. It costs 2.75 per month per unit to store and insure the commodity. If interest rates are currently 6.40%, what is a fair five-month forward price?

b. Suppose you are an end user of the commodity and require delivery of the commodity in five months. If the price of a five-month futures contract is currently 496.00, what would you do?

c. If the price of the same five-month futures contract is currently 480.00, now what would you, as an end user, do?

d. The additional amount that buyers are willing to pay right now for immediate access to a commodity is sometimes referred to as the convenience yield. Using the interest rate and storage costs in the previous question, if the commodity is still trading at a cash price of 463.25 and a two-month futures contract is trading at a price of 468.50, what is the two-month convenience yield?

6. If S is the current exchange rate for a foreign currency (the foreign currency in domestic currency units), t is the time to maturity, r_d is the domestic currency interest rate, and r_f is the foreign currency interest rate, then, using simple interest, the forward price F for a foreign currency can be approximated as:

$$F = S \times (1 + r_d t) / (1 + r_f t)$$

Suppose that at the current exchange rate one British pound is equal to 1.24 euros (£1.00 = €1.24). If the pound interest rate is 3.78% and the euro interest rate is 2.32%, what should be a three-month forward price for the pound expressed in euros?

CHAPTER 3

Contract Specifications and Terminology

1. When a stock option is exercised, regardless of the current stock price, the underlying stock is bought or sold at a price equal to the exercise price.

   If the underlying contract is 100 shares of stock, what is the stock position (+ for long, – for short) and cash flow (+ for a credit, – for a debit) resulting from each of the following actions?

	ACTION	STOCK PRICE	STOCK POSITION	CASH FLOW
a.	you exercise 2 February 70 calls	73.50		
b.	you exercise 8 April 40 puts	35.25		
c.	you are assigned on 16 June 55 calls	58.10		
d.	you are assigned on 5 August 120 puts	116.85		
e.	you exercise 37 October 25 puts	25.00		
f.	you are assigned on 21 December 160 calls	183.00		

2. If the underlying contract is 100 shares of stock, what will be your total stock position and cash flow if all of the following occur?

ACTION	STOCK POSITION	CASH FLOW
you exercise 25 August 75 calls		
you exercise 42 August 95 puts		
you are assigned on 16 August 80 calls		
you are assigned on 51 August 100 puts		
totals		

3. When an option on a futures contract is exercised, the underlying futures contract is bought or sold at the exercise price, and the position is immediately subject to futures-type settlement. Consequently there will be an immediate variation credit or debit equal to the difference between the current futures price and the exercise price.

If the underlying is a futures contract, what is the futures position (+ for long, – for short) and cash flow (+ for a credit, – for a debit) resulting from each of the following actions?

	ACTION	FUTURES PRICE	FUTURES POINT VALUE	FUTURES POSITION	CASH FLOW
a.	you exercise 10 January 1300 calls	1325.00	100		
b.	you are assigned 3 March 95 calls	98.50	1,000		
c.	you exercise on 21 May 1850 puts	1832.50	250		
d.	you are assigned on 65 July 900 puts	866.50	10		
e.	you exercise 48 September 650 calls	650.00	50		
f.	you are assigned on 30 December 150 puts	137.50	500		

4. For futures options, when there is no listed futures month with the same month designation as the option expiration month, the underlying futures contract for the option is the nearest listed futures month beyond the option expiration month.

Suppose underlying futures contracts are listed for March, June, September, and December. What will be the futures position resulting from each of the following actions?

	ACTION	FUTURES POSITION
a.	You exercise 7 October 100 calls	
b.	You are assigned on 4 February 40 puts	
c.	You exercise 11 September 250 puts	
d.	You are assigned on 20 May 75 calls	

e. With the same four listed futures months (March, June, September, December), March futures are trading at 1,378.90 and June futures are trading at 1,384.60. If each point has a value of 200, what will be your total futures position and cash flow if all of the following occur?

ACTION	FUTURES POSITION	CASH FLOW
you exercise 26 March 1350 calls		
you exercise 17 April 1,425 puts		
you are assigned 9 April 1375 calls		
you are assigned on 40 February 1400 puts		
totals		

5. When an option on a cash index is exercised, no underlying position results. But there is a cash payment equal to the difference between the exercise price and the current index price.

   If the underlying is a cash index, what is the underlying position (+ for long, – for short) and cash flow (+ for a credit, – for a debit) resulting from each of the following actions?

	ACTION	INDEX PRICE	INDEX POINT VALUE	UNDERLYING POSITION	CASH FLOW
a.	you exercise 10 March 5000 calls	5,353.63	10		
b.	you are assigned 7 June 2400 puts	2,318.35	500		
c.	you exercise on 21 September 1850 puts	1,832.48	250		
d.	you are assigned on 36 December 3900 calls	4,254.11	100		

6. An option's price is always made up specifically of its intrinsic value and time value, where call intrinsic value = maximum of [0, underlying price – exercise price] put intrinsic value = maximum of [0, exercise price – underlying price]

   For each option price and underlying price below, what is the intrinsic value and time value?

	OPTION	OPTION PRICE	UNDERLYING PRICE	INTRINSIC VALUE	TIME VALUE
a.	January 90 call	4.75	85.00		
b.	March 75 put	4.70	71.60		
c.	May 125 call	22.25	147.25		

(continued on next page)

	OPTION	OPTION PRICE	UNDERLYING PRICE	INTRINSIC VALUE	TIME VALUE
d.	July 40 put	1.35	45.65		
e.	September 1300 call	31.80	1,303.25		
f.	November 600 put	71.50	528.50		
g.	February 2500 call	67.25	2,491.00		
h.	April 250 put	20.15	231.15		
i.	June 15 call	.95	15.10		
j.	August 5500 put	650.00	4,850.00		
k.	October 32.50 call	1.10	33.45		
l.	December 100 put	9.80	93.90		

7. The type of option is either a call or a put. For each option below, fill in the missing value or option type.

	UNDERLYING PRICE	EXERCISE PRICE	OPTION TYPE	OPTION PRICE	INTRINSIC VALUE	TIME VALUE
a.		70	call	6.75	4.10	
b.	78.15		call	4.55		1.40
c.	73.65	80			6.35	.75
d.	64.90		put	6.00	5.10	
e.		60	call		11.50	.50
f.	68.50	65	put	2.50		
g.	891.20		call	22.45		6.25
h.	817.90	825			7.10	10.00
i.		850	call	33.75		7.50
j.	866.25		put		33.75	3.10
k.	796.40	800		12.75	0	
l.		925	put		50.00	2.50

8. An option is in-the-money if intrinsic value > 0.

An option is out-of-the-money if intrinsic value ≤ 0.

An option is at-the-money if exercise price = current underlying price (a special case of out-of-the-money).

For each option and underlying price below, is the option in-the-money or out-of-the-money, and by how much?

	OPTION	UNDERLYING PRICE	IN-THE-MONEY OR OUT-OF-THE-MONEY	BY HOW MUCH?
a.	March 75 call	81.50		
b.	July 2300 put	2,475.00		
c.	November 650 call	648.00		
d.	February 17.50 put	17.35		
e.	June 130 call	165.25		
f.	October 117 put	117.66		

9. Options are currently listed for trading at the following exercise prices.

45, 50, 55, 60, 65, 70, 75

At the underlying prices below, which call and put is closest to at-the-money? Which calls and puts are in-the-money?

	UNDERLYING PRICE	EXERCISE PRICE THAT IS CLOSEST TO AT-THE-MONEY	EXERCISE PRICES FOR WHICH CALLS ARE IN-THE-MONEY	EXERCISE PRICES FOR WHICH PUTS ARE IN-THE-MONEY
a.	55.00			
b.	64.50			
c.	51.75			
d.	67.00			

10. At an underlying price of 101.90, what is the intrinsic value and time value for calls and puts at each of the following expiration months and exercise prices?

OPTION	CALL PRICE	CALL INTRINSIC VALUE	CALL TIME VALUE	PUT PRICE	PUT INTRINSIC VALUE	PUT TIME VALUE
April 80	23.00			.50		
April 85	18.25			.70		
April 90	13.60			1.20		
April 95	9.65			2.15		
April 100	6.15			3.65		
April 105	3.60			6.10		

(continued on next page)

OPTION	CALL PRICE	CALL INTRINSIC VALUE	CALL TIME VALUE	PUT PRICE	PUT INTRINSIC VALUE	PUT TIME VALUE
April 110	2.00			9.50		
April 115	1.05			13.75		
April 120	.65			18.25		
May 80	24.25			1.25		
May 85	19.80			1.80		
May 90	15.75			2.70		
May 95	12.25			4.00		
May 100	9.10			6.00		
May 105	6.50			8.50		
May 110	4.50			11.50		
May 115	3.15			15.15		
May 120	2.10			19.15		

From your answers in the table which option—in-the-money, at-the-money, or out-of-the-money—carries the greatest amount of time value?

Which option—in-the-money, at-the-money, or out-of-the-money—carries the least amount of time value?

CHAPTER 4

Expiration Profit and Loss

1. Using the grid below, draw the parity graphs (the value at expiration) for the following positions:

    a. long a 65 call

    b. short a 70 call

    c. long a 75 put

    d. short an 80 put

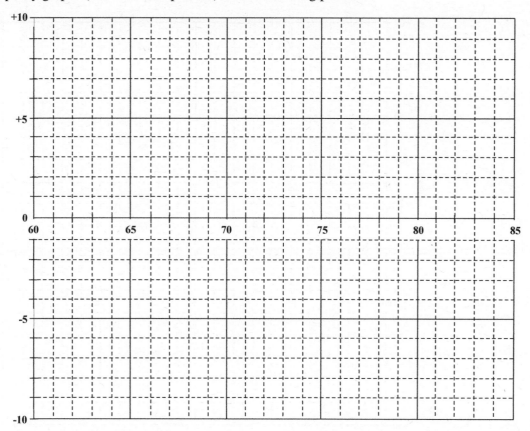

2. Using the grid below, draw the parity graphs (the value at expiration) for the following combination positions:

a. long a 70 put and long a 75 call

b. long an 80 put and short an 80 call

c. short two 65 calls

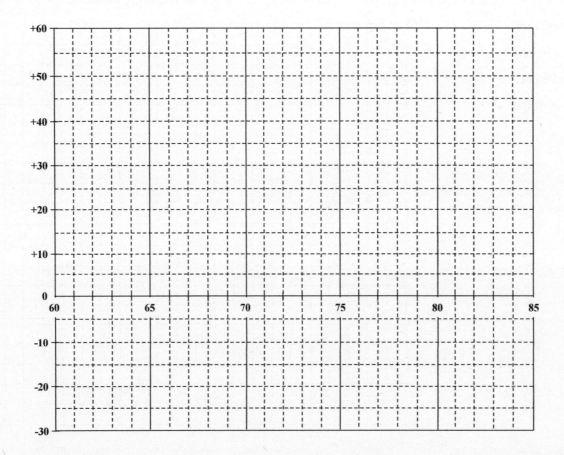

3. The slopes of the various option and underlying positions at expiration can be summarized as follows:

POSITION	SLOPE
long an underlying contract	+1
long an in-the-money call	+1
short an in-the-money put	+1
short an underlying contract	−1
short an in-the-money call	−1
long an in-the-money put	−1
long or short an out-of-the money option	0

For each position below, what is the slope of the expiration graph over the given underlying price intervals? From these slopes, sketch the shape of the expiration P&L graph. (The sketch need not be to scale—the approximate shape is sufficient.)

	POSITION	UNDERLYING PRICE	SLOPE	SKETCH
a.	long 2 January 70 calls	below 70		
		above 70		
b.	short 3 February 65 puts	below 65		
		above 65		
c.	long 4 March 75 puts	below 75		
		above 75		

(continued on next page)

	POSITION	UNDERLYING PRICE	SLOPE	SKETCH
d.	short 9 April 60 calls	below 60		
		above 60		
e.	long 2 May 70 calls	below 70		
	long 2 May 70 puts	above 70		
f.	long 2 June 70 calls	below 65		
	short 2 June 65 puts	between 65 and 70		
		above 70		
g.	short 5 July 75 calls	below 75		
	long 5 July 75 puts	above 75		
h.	short 10 August 70 calls	below 70		
	long 5 underlying contracts	above 70		
i.	long 3 September 70 calls	below 65		
	short 3 September 65 puts	between 65 and 70		
	short 3 underlying contracts	above 70		

(continued on next page)

	POSITION	UNDERLYING PRICE	SLOPE	SKETCH
j.	short 4 October 60 calls	below 60		
	short 3 October 75 puts	between 60 and 75		
	long 4 underlying contracts	above 75		
k.	long 5 November 65 calls	below 65		
	short 8 November 65 puts	between 65 and 70		
	long 4 November 70 calls	between 70 and 75		
	long 9 November 75 puts	above 75		
l.	long 7 December 60 puts	below 60		
	short 3 December 65 calls	between 60 and 65		
	short 8 December 70 puts	between 65 and 70		
	short 5 underlying contracts	above 70		

4. Using the underlying price and option prices below, draw the expiration profit and loss graph for the given positions. What are the breakeven prices for each position?

underlying price = 72.00

MARCH OPTIONS	65	70	75	80
calls	9.00	5.50	3.00	1.50
puts	1.00	2.50	4.75	8.25

a. long a March 70 call

b. short a March 65 put

c. long a March 75 put

d. short a March 80 call

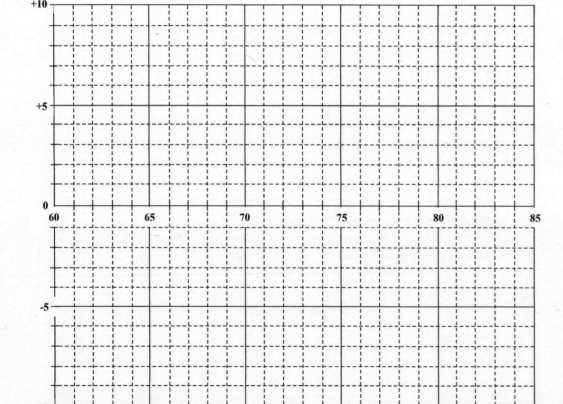

e. long a March 70 call and short a March 80 call

f. long a March 80 put and short 2 March 70 puts

g. short a March 70 call and long a March 70 put

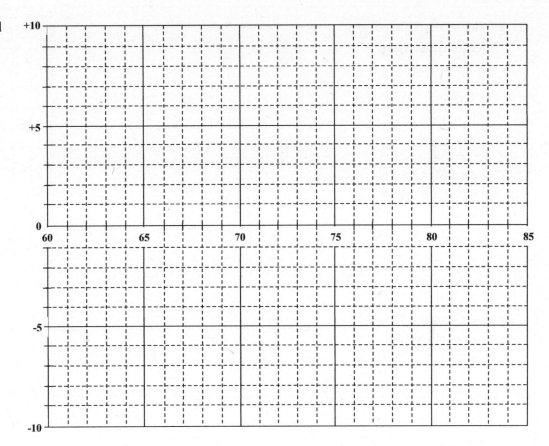

h. long a March 70 put and long an underlying contract

i. long a March 65 put and short a March 75 call

j. long a March 70 call and long a March 70 put

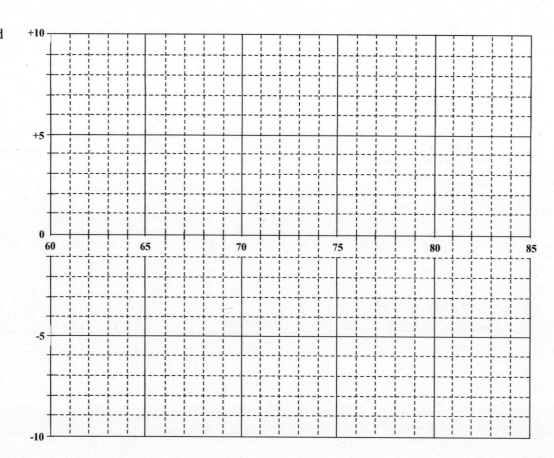

5. You have the position and contract prices shown in the following chart.

    a. What will be your profit or loss if the underlying contract at expiration is trading at a price of 70.00?

CONTRACT POSITION	CONTRACT PRICE	CONTRACT VALUE AT 70.00	TOTAL CONTRACT PROFIT OR LOSS
−4 March 70 calls	6.00		
−5 March 70 puts	3.25		
+6 March 75 calls	4.50		
+8 March 75 puts	2.00		
+6 underlying contracts	73.00		
Total P&L at 70.00			

    b. What is the expiration slope of your position . . .

	PRICE	EXPIRATION SLOPE
i.	below 70?	
ii.	between 70 and 75?	
iii.	above 75?	

c. Using the slopes of your position and the P&L at 70.00, what will be your profit or loss at expiration at the following underlying prices?

	UNDERLYING PRICE	PROFIT OR LOSS AT EXPIRATION
i.	65.00	
ii.	75.00	
iii.	85.00	

d. To the nearest .01, what are the breakeven prices for the entire position?

e. On the following grid, draw the value of your position at expiration.

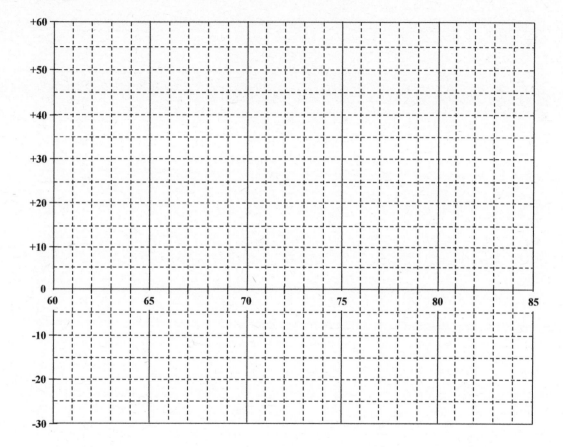

CHAPTER 5

Theoretical Evaluation

In an arbitrage-free market, where no arbitrage profit is available, the expected value for a contract at maturity (its average value at maturity) must be equal to its forward price.

1. The following diagram represents the price distribution and associated probabilities for an underlying contract three months from now.

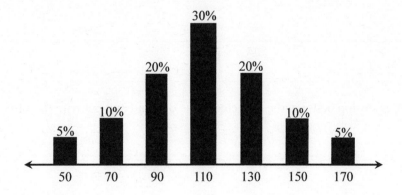

   a. If there is no arbitrage opportunity, what should be the three-month forward price for the underlying contract?

b. What are the expected values for the following options?

	OPTION	EXPECTED VALUE
i.	70 call	
ii.	70 put	
iii.	110 call	
iv.	110 put	
v.	135 call	
vi.	135 put	

c. Can you identify a relationship between the expected value of a call and put with the same exercise price?

d. The theoretical value of an option is the present value of its expected value at expiration.

If all options are European and subject to stock-type settlement, there are three months to expiration, and annual interest rates are 6.00%, to the nearest .01 what is the theoretical value of each option?

	OPTION	THEORETICAL VALUE
i.	70 call	
ii.	70 put	
iii.	110 call	
iv.	110 put	
v.	135 call	
vi.	135 put	

e. Suppose the underlying contract is a stock that is expected to pay a dividend of .75 over the next three months. Ignoring interest on dividends, to the nearest .01 what should be the current price of the stock?

2. The following diagram represents the probability and price distribution for an underlying stock six months from now.

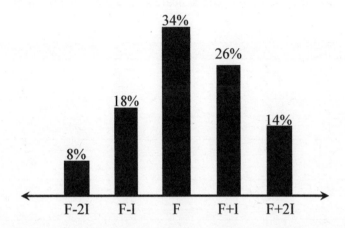

a. If the stock is currently trading at a price of 72.50, annual interest rates are 8%, and the stock pays no dividend, to the nearest .01 what is the stock's six-month forward price, *F*?

b. Suppose we assign a value of 5.00 to each interval, I. What are the stock prices, $F - 2I$ through $F + 2I$, on the above probability distribution?

F − 2I	F − I	F	F + I	F + 2I

c. Using these price intervals, what is the expected value for the underlying stock?

d. Given the forward price and expected value for the underlying stock, what strategy might you pursue?

e. If all options are European and subject to stock-type settlement, there are six months to expiration, and annual interest rates are 8.00%, to the nearest .01 what is the expected value and theoretical value of each option?

i.	70 call	expected value = theoretical value =
ii.	70 put	expected value = theoretical value =
iii.	80 call	expected value = theoretical value =
iv.	80 put	expected value = theoretical value =

3. In question 1c the following relationship seemed to be true:

call expected value – put expected value = forward price – exercise price

a. Using the values in question 2, does this relationship still hold true? If not, is there an alternative relationship?

b. What annual interest rate will result in the six-month forward price for the stock being equal to the stock's expected value?

c. Suppose we increase the value of *I* in question 2 to 10.00. What are the new underlying prices, *F* – 2*I* through *F* + 2*I*, on the above probability distribution?

F – 2I	*F – I*	*F*	*F + I*	*F + 2I*

d. What is the expected value for the underlying contract?

e. If all options are European and subject to stock-type settlement, there are six months to expiration, and annual interest rates are 8.00%, to the nearest .01 what is the expected value and theoretical value of each option?

i.	70 call	expected value = theoretical value =
ii.	70 put	expected value = theoretical value =
iii.	80 call	expected value = theoretical value =
iv.	80 put	expected value = theoretical value =

f. Now what is the relationship between the expected value of a call and put at the same exercise price?

CHAPTER 6

Volatility

1. If t is a time period expressed in years, σ is the annual volatility, and F is the forward or futures price, then for simple volatility calculations (rather than exponential calculations) a price change of n standard deviations over the time period t can be approximated as:

$$n \times F \times \sigma \times \sqrt{t}$$

For a daily standard deviation, traders customarily assume 256 trading days in a year.

t is therefore 1/256, and $\sqrt{t} = 1/16$

For a weekly standard deviation, assuming 52 trading weeks in a year, t is 1/52, and $\sqrt{t} \approx 1/7.2$.

Using simple volatility calculations, and assuming that the forward price is equal to the current price, what is an approximate daily and weekly one standard deviation price change for each of the contracts below?

a. contract price = 78.00

VOLATILITY	20%	30%	40%	50%
daily standard deviation				
weekly standard deviation				

b. contract price = 1,325.00

VOLATILITY	10%	15%	20%	25%
daily standard deviation				
weekly standard deviation				

c. contract price = 1.6270

VOLATILITY	8%	10%	12%	14%
daily standard deviation				
weekly standard deviation				

d. contract price = 669.00

VOLATILITY	15%	23%	31%	39%
daily standard deviation				
weekly standard deviation				

e. contract price = 3,187.00

VOLATILITY	13%	17%	21%	25%
daily standard deviation				
weekly standard deviation				

2. Using simple volatility calculations, for each futures contract and volatility below, what is an approximate one and two standard deviation price range over the given time period? Assume that a year is made up of 12 months, 52 weeks, or 365 days.

	FUTURES PRICE	VOLATILITY	TIME PERIOD	DOWN ONE ST. DEV.	UP ONE ST. DEV.	DOWN TWO ST. DEVS.	UP TWO ST. DEVS.
a.	226.00	21%	14 weeks				
b.	1,869.00	14%	11 months				
c.	103.82	9.5%	116 days				
d.	16.97	38%	5 months				
e.	9,623	18.25%	23 weeks				

3. To calculate a more exact price change, we can use the exponential function e^x or $\exp(x)$. If F is the forward or futures price, t is a time period expressed in years, and σ is the annual volatility:

$$\text{up } n \text{ standard deviations} = F \times e^{n\sigma\sqrt{t}}$$

$$\text{down } n \text{ standard deviations} = F \times e^{-n\sigma\sqrt{t}}$$

Using the same prices, volatilities, and time periods in question 2, recalculate the one and two standard deviation price ranges using the exponential function. How do these values differ from the simple values above?

	FUTURES PRICE	VOLATILITY	TIME PERIOD	DOWN ONE ST. DEV.	UP ONE ST. DEV.	DOWN TWO ST. DEVS.	UP TWO ST. DEVS.
a.	226.00	21%	14 weeks				
b.	1,869.00	14%	11 months				
c.	103.82	9.5%	116 days				
d.	16.97	38%	5 months				
e.	9,623	18.25%	23 weeks				

4. A stock that is currently trading at a price of 104.75 has a volatility of 27.42%.

a. What is a one and two standard deviation price range 192 days from now if interest rates are 6.19% and the stock is expected to pay total dividends of 2.28 over this period? For this question use simple interest and volatility calculations and ignore any interest on dividends.

b. Suppose the dividend of 2.28 will be paid all at once in 43 days. Now go back and do the same one and two standard deviation calculation using continuous interest and volatility (the exponential function), and include any interest that can be earned on the dividend. Assume that the same interest rate of 6.19% applies to all interest calculations.

5. For a normal distribution, the following are the approximate probabilities associated with one, two, and three standard deviations:

- a move greater than one standard deviation, in either direction: 31¾ %
- a move greater than two standard deviations, in either direction: 4½ %
- a move greater than three standard deviations, in either direction: ¼ %

a. Using the above values, fill in the probabilities indicated by the question marks in the following drawing (the percentage of the area under the normal distribution curve between each set of dotted lines).

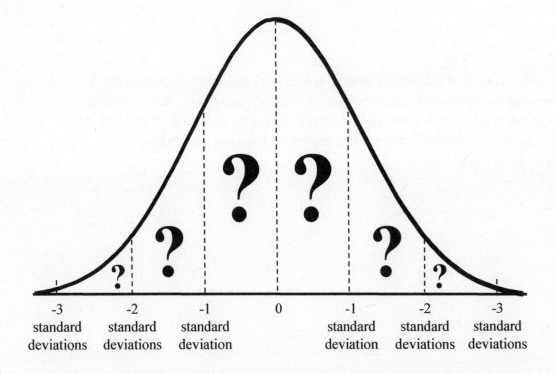

| -3 standard deviations | -2 standard deviations | -1 standard deviation | 0 | -1 standard deviation | -2 standard deviations | -3 standard deviations |

b. From your answers above, what is the approximate probability of getting an occurrence over the following ranges?

   i. An up move less than two standard deviations

   ii. An up or down move between one and two standard deviations

  iii. A down move between two and three standard deviations

   iv. An up move of less than one standard deviation or a down move of less than two standard deviations.

v. A down move between one and two standard deviations and an up move between two and three standard deviations

vi. A down move greater than two standard deviations and an up move greater than one standard deviation

vii. An up move greater than three standard deviations

6. An underlying contract is trading at a price close to 100. The implied volatility of options in this market is approximately 20%. Over a 10-day period you observe the following 10 close-to-close price changes for the underlying contract:

DAY 1	up	.75
DAY 2	down	2.40
DAY 3	up	1.75
DAY 4	up	.40
DAY 5	up	3.20
DAY 6	down	1.55
DAY 7	down	1.00
DAY 8	up	.15
DAY 9	up	1.40
DAY 10	down	.55

a. Do you think these price changes are consistent with a volatility of 20%? If not, why?

b. If 20% seems wrong, using only a simple calculator, what might be your volatility estimate for the 10-day period?

CHAPTER 7

Risk Measurement

1. Match each risk measure with the correct definition:

RISK MEASURE	DEFINITION
1. theta	**A.** The sensitivity of an option's theoretical value to a change in volatility
2. gamma	**B.** The sensitivity of an option's theoretical value to a change in the underlying price
3. rho	**C.** The sensitivity of an option's delta to a change in the underlying price
4. vega	**D.** The sensitivity of an option's theoretical value to a change in interest rates
5. delta	**E.** The sensitivity of an option's theoretical value to the passage of time

2. For stock options, which risk measure can be used to estimate the sensitivity of an option's value to a change in the dividend?

3. For each option value and delta below, to the nearest .01 estimate the option's new value if the underlying price changes by the given amount.

	CURRENT OPTION VALUE	DELTA (WHOLE NUMBER FORMAT)	UNDERLYING PRICE CHANGE	NEW OPTION VALUE
a.	10.25	60	+.40	
b.	24.60	−44	−5.20	
c.	5.41	27	−2.30	
d.	51.40	−15	+13.68	
e.	1.24	72	+.18	
f.	8.90	−85	−5.25	

Which of the above options are calls, and which are puts?

4. As the underlying price changes, the delta will change by an amount indicated by the gamma, where the gamma is expressed as the change in the delta per one point change in the underlying price. To approximate the change in an option's value as the underlying price changes, we can use the average delta for the given price change.

For each option delta and gamma below, estimate the option's new delta if the underlying price changes by the given amount. Then, using the option's average delta, to the nearest .01 estimate the option's new value if the underlying price changes by the given amount. (Delta and gamma are both given in the whole number format.)

	CURRENT OPTION VALUE	DELTA	GAMMA	UNDERLYING PRICE CHANGE	NEW OPTION DELTA	NEW OPTION VALUE
a.	4.58	57	4	+3.00		
b.	1.70	−39	7	−.94		
c.	4.94	28	1.1	−8.50		
d.	10.09	−83	2.8	−6.75		
e.	.58	21	6.5	−3.70		
f.	3.95	−12	.3	+18.20		

5. Theta is usually expressed as the change in an option's value per one day's passage of time.

Vega is usually expressed as the change in an option's value per one percentage point change in volatility.

Rho is usually expressed as the change in an option's value per one percentage point change in interest rates.

For each option value, risk measure, and change in market conditions below, to the nearest .01 estimate the option's new value.

	OPTION VALUE	RISK MEASURE	CHANGE IN MARKET CONDITIONS	NEW OPTION VALUE
a.	5.18	theta = −.095	2 days pass	
b.	.67	vega = .047	volatility rises 3.2%	
c.	22.75	rho = −.177	interest rates rise 2.90%	
d.	1.64	theta = −.024	13 days pass	
e.	12.10	vega = .232	volatility falls 5.6%	
f.	3.99	rho = .088	interest rates fall 1.67%	

6. For each option and set of risk measures below, to the nearest .01 what will be the option's new price if the given changes in market conditions occur?

a. current option price = 4.55
delta = 62 (whole number format)
gamma = 4.4 (whole number format)
vega = .13

The underlying price falls by 3.28 and implied volatility rises by 2.6 percentage points.

b. current option price = 8.87
theta = −.199
rho = −.135

Six days pass with no change in the underlying price and interest rates fall 1.20 percentage points (120 basis points).

c. current option price = 4.73

   delta = 43 (whole number format)

   vega = .217

   theta = −.027

   rho = .142

Four days pass, implied volatility falls 1.75 percentage points, interest rates rise .75 percentage points, and the dividend is increased by .37 (this is a stock option).

7. Complete each of the following statements:

   a. A position with a positive delta wants _____

   b. A position with a negative gamma wants _____

   c. A position with a negative rho wants _____

   d. A position with a positive vega wants _____

   e. A position with a positive gamma wants _____

   f. A position with a positive delta and negative gamma wants _____

8. Complete each statement below with either "increase in value" or "decline in value."

   a. If the underlying price remains unchanged, as time passes a position with a negative theta will

   _____

   b. If the underlying price remains unchanged, as time passes a position with a positive gamma will

   _____

   c. If interest rates fall, a position with a negative rho will _____

   d. If implied volatility falls, a position with a negative vega will _____

   e. If the underlying price makes a large move, a position with a positive theta will _____

   f. If the underlying price makes a large move, a position with a positive gamma will _____

9. Fill in each blank with either "long" or "short."

   a. A trader who buys calls has a _____ theta position.

   b. A trader who sells puts has a _____ delta position.

   c. A trader who sells puts has a _____ gamma position.

   d. A trader who sells calls has a _____ vega position.

   e. A trader who buys stock option puts has a _____ rho position.

   f. A trader who sells puts has a _____ theta position.

   g. A trader who buys puts has a _____ vega position.

   h. A trader who sells stock option calls has a _____ rho position.

   i. A trader who buys calls has a _____ gamma position.

10. Match each set of risk measures below with the set of conditions that will most work in the position's favor.

RISK MEASURES	FAVORABLE CHANGES IN MARKET CONDITIONS
1. positive delta negative gamma negative vega positive rho	**A.** swift upward price move indifferent to changes in implied volatility falling interest rates
2. zero delta positive gamma negative vega negative rho	**B.** downward price movement indifferent to changes in implied volatility indifferent to changes in interest rates
3. negative delta negative gamma positive vega positive rho	**C.** slow upward price movement falling implied volatility rising interest rates
4. positive delta positive gamma zero vega negative rho	**D.** swift price move in either direction falling implied volatility falling interest rates
5. negative delta zero gamma zero vega zero rho	**E.** slow downward price movement rising implied volatility rising interest rates

11.

OPTION	DELTA	GAMMA	THETA	VEGA	RHO
June 65 call	79	4.2	−.0190	.100	.121
June 70 call	52	5.8	−.0205	.137	.083
June 75 call	26	4.7	−.0152	.112	.043
June 65 put	−21	4.2	−.0084	.100	−.039
June 70 put	−48	5.8	−.0092	.137	−.089
June 75 put	−74	4.7	−.0030	.112	−.142

From the evaluation table above, a trader has the following position:

+3 underlying contracts

+5 June 65 calls   −8 June 65 puts

−6 June 70 calls   −11 June 70 puts

−14 June 75 calls   +6 June 75 puts

a. What is the trader's total . . .

  i. delta position? _____

  ii. gamma position? _____

iii. theta position? _____

iv. vega position? _____

v. rho position? _____

b. Describe the changes in market conditions that will most help the position.

c. Suppose that based on your assumptions about market conditions your entire position has a positive theoretical edge of 4.65 (you expect to show a profit of 4.65). What will be your theoretical edge if all of the following occur?

the underlying price rises 3.50

three days pass

you raise your volatility estimate by 2.40 percentage points

you reduce your estimate of interest rates by .50% (50 basis points)

| CHAPTER 8 |

Delta Neutral Positions and Dynamic Hedging

1. The process of delta hedging an option position to remain delta neutral is an important part of using a theoretical pricing model. In a delta neutral position all the deltas add up to approximately zero, or at least as close to zero as is practically possible.

	JULY 70	JULY 80	JULY 90
call delta	70	41	18
put delta	−30	−59	−82

a. You buy 25 July 80 calls. From the table of delta values above, what do you need to do (buy? sell? how many?) to hedge your position as close to delta neutral as possible using each of the following contracts?

i.	underlying contract		
ii.	July 90 call		
iii.	July 80 put		

b. You sell 50 July 70 puts. What do you need to do (buy? sell? how many?) to hedge your position as close to delta neutral as possible using each of the following contracts:

i.	July 70 call		
ii.	July 80 put		
iii.	July 90 put		

c. You sell 15 underlying contracts. You would like to hedge half your delta position using July 80 puts and the other half using July 90 calls. As close as possible, how many of each contract do you need to buy or to sell?

2. In each of the option positions below, how many underlying contracts do you need to buy or sell in order to create an initial delta neutral position? Then, as the delta changes, how many underlying contracts do you need to buy or sell in order to maintain a delta neutral position, or a position that is as close to delta neutral as possible? Delta values are given in the whole number format.

a. long 10 calls

CURRENT OPTION DELTA	CURRENT TOTAL DELTA POSITION	UNDERLYING CONTRACTS TO BUY OR SELL
70		
50		
40		
80		

b. short 30 calls

OPTION DELTA	DELTA POSITION	UNDERLYING CONTRACTS TO BUY OR SELL
28		
40		
63		
52		

c. long 62 puts

OPTION DELTA	CURRENT TOTAL DELTA POSITION	UNDERLYING CONTRACTS TO BUY OR SELL
−65		
−71		
−33		
−49		

d. short 44 puts

OPTION DELTA	CURRENT TOTAL DELTA POSITION	UNDERLYING CONTRACTS TO BUY OR SELL
−95		
−77		
−40		
0		

3. In theory an option's value should be equal to the present value of its intrinsic value at expiration, plus the present value of all the cash flows resulting from the delta neutral dynamic hedging process.

In the two scenarios below, assume that the option is hedged at each given underlying price and delta. If interest rates are zero (no present valuing is necessary), what are the values of each option?

a. 55 call

UNDERLYING PRICE	DELTA (WHOLE NUMBER FORMAT)	HEDGE	CASH FLOW	TOTAL HEDGE
53.70 (initial)	45 (initial)			
55.70	57			
53.40	40			
57.10	69			
55.00	51			
51.50 (underlying price at expiration)				

b. 70 put

UNDERLYING PRICE	DELTA (WHOLE NUMBER FORMAT)	HEDGE	CASH FLOW	TOTAL HEDGE
68.42 (initial)	−65 (initial)			
69.71	−52			
71.29	−33			
70.19	−46			
71.02	−28			
68.51 (underlying price at expiration)				

CHAPTER 9

The Dynamics of Risk

Nothing in option markets remains constant. Not only are theoretical values constantly changing as market conditions change, but the risk sensitivities are also changing. Understanding how the sensitivities change as market conditions change is an important part of an active option trader's education.

Following are some important principles of risk dynamics:

- An at-the-money option (or, more correctly, an at-the-forward option) has a greater gamma, theta, and vega than a similar in- or out-of-the-money option.
- As volatility increases, call deltas move toward 50, and put deltas move toward –50.
- As volatility declines or time passes, call deltas move away from 50, and put deltas move away from –50.
- As volatility increases, the gamma of at-the-money options decline, while the gamma of in-the-money and out-of-the money options increase.
- As volatility declines or time passes, the gamma of at-the-money options increase, while gamma of in-the-money and out-of-the money options decline.
- As volatility rises, the theta of all options will increase. (The option has more value to lose over an equal amount of time.)
- As volatility falls, the theta of all options will decline. (The option has less value to lose over an equal amount of time.)
- As volatility changes, the vega of an at-the-money option will remain essentially unchanged.
- As time passes, the theta of an at-the-money option increases.
- As time passes, the vega of all options declines.
- If an option has a nonzero rho value, as time passes the rho will decline.
- If an option has a nonzero rho value, the greater the value of the option, the greater the rho.

1. An underlying contract is currently trading at a price of 75. If there are no interest considerations (interest rates are zero), for each pair of options choose the correct answer.

    a. If the underlying price changes, but all other market conditions remain unchanged, which option's price will change the most?

       i. a 1-month 75 call   **ii.** a 1-month 75 put   **iii.** a 1-month 80 put
            a 1-month 80 call   a 1-month 80 put   a 3-month 80 put

    b. If the underlying price changes, but all other market conditions remain unchanged, which option's delta will change the most?

       i. a 1-month 75 call   **ii.** a 1-month 75 call   **iii.** a 1-month 65 put
            a 1-month 80 call   a 3-month 75 call   a 3-month 65 put

    c. If the implied volatility changes by the same amount for all options, but all other market conditions remain unchanged, which option's price will change the most?

       i. a 3-month 70 put   **ii.** a 1-month 75 put   **iii.** a 1-month 85 call
            a 3-month 75 put   a 3-month 75 put   a 3-month 85 call

    d. If two weeks pass with no change in the price of the underlying contract, but all other market conditions remain unchanged, which option's price will change the most?

       i. a 1-month 70 call   **ii.** a 1-month 75 call   **iii.** a 1-month 65 put
            a 1-month 75 call   a 3-month 75 call   a 3-month 65 put

    e. If the underlying contract is stock, and interest rates change by the same amount for all expiration months, but all other market conditions remain unchanged, which option's price will change the most?

       i. a 3-month 70 call   **ii.** a 1-month 80 call   **iii.** a 1-month 70 put
            a 3-month 75 call   a 3-month 80 call   a 1-month 75 put

f. If the underlying contract is a stock that is expected to pay a dividend in two months, if the dividend is changed but all other market conditions remain unchanged, which option's price will change the most?

    i. a 3-month 70 call   **ii.** a 1-month 80 call   **iii.** a 3-month 75 put

        a 3-month 75 call   a 3-month 80 call   a 3-month 80 put

2. For each option below, with the given change in market conditions is each risk measure (delta, gamma, theta, vega), in absolute value, getting bigger (+), smaller (–), or staying about the same (0)?

    underlying price = 50

    time to expiration = 3 months

    interest rate = 0

a. The underlying price falls to 45

	DELTA	GAMMA	THETA	VEGA
40 call				
50 call				
60 call				
40 put				
50 put				
60 put				

b. The underlying price rises to 55

	DELTA	GAMMA	THETA	VEGA
40 call				
50 call				
60 call				
40 put				
50 put				
60 put				

c. Two weeks pass

	DELTA	GAMMA	THETA	VEGA
40 call				
50 call				
60 call				
40 put				
50 put				
60 put				

d. Volatility falls

	DELTA	GAMMA	THETA	VEGA
40 call				
50 call				
60 call				
40 put				
50 put				
60 put				

e. Volatility rises

	DELTA	GAMMA	THETA	VEGA
40 call				
50 call				
60 call				
40 put				
50 put				
60 put				

Higher order risk measures (the sensitivity of a sensitivity) are sometimes used to approximate how basic risk measures (delta, gamma, theta, vega) will change as market conditions change. Some higher order risk measures:

Vanna—the sensitivity of the delta to a change in volatility (delta change per one percentage point change in volatility), or, the sensitivity of the vega to a change in underlying price (vega change per 1.00 change in the underlying price)

Charm—the sensitivity of the delta to the passage of time (delta change per one day passage of time), or the sensitivity of the theta to a change in underlying price (theta change per 1.00 change in the underlying price)

Volga—the sensitivity of the vega to a change in volatility (vega change per 1% change in volatility)

Vega decay—the sensitivity of the vega to the passage of time (vega change per one day passage of time)

Speed—the sensitivity of the gamma to a change in underlying price (gamma change per 1.00 change).

Color—the sensitivity of the gamma to the passage of time (gamma change per one day passage of time)

underlying stock price = 100

time to expiration = 3 months

Interest rate = 6.00%

volatility = 20%

	TH. VALUE	DELTA	GAMMA	THETA	VEGA	VANNA	CHARM	VOLGA	VEGA DECAY	SPEED	COLOR
90 call	11.86	.895	.018	−.0227	.091	−.010	.0009	.0066	−.0010	−.0025	0
100 call	4.74	.579	.039	−.0302	.195	−.002	−.0004	.0002	−.0010	−.0012	.0002
110 call	1.24	.225	.030	−.0200	.150	.013	−.0019	.0048	−.0015	.0020	0
90 put	.52	−.105	.018	−.0082	.091	−.010	.0009	.0066	−.0010	−.0025	0
100 put	3.25	−.421	.039	−.0140	.195	−.002	−.0004	.0002	−.0010	−.0012	.0002
110 put	9.61	−.775	.030	−.0022	.150	.013	−.0019	.0048	−.0015	.0020	0

In the above table, and for purposes of this exercise, the delta and gamma values are expressed in the decimal format. Delta values for calls range from 0 to 1.00, and for puts from 0 to −1.00.

3. Using the table of values above, try to answer the following questions:

a.	If volatility falls to 18%, what will be the new delta values of the 90 call and the 100 put?	
b.	If 10 days pass, what will be the new delta values of the 90 put and the 100 call?	
c.	If 10 days pass, what will be the new gamma values of the 90 call and the 100 put?	
d.	If the underlying price falls to 96, what will be the new vega values of the 90 put and the 110 call?	
e.	If the underlying price rises to 103, what will be the new theta values of the 90 call and the 110 put?	
f.	If ten days pass, what will be the new vega values of the 100 call and 110 put?	
g.	If volatility rises to 25%, what will be the new vega values of the 90 put and the 110 call?	

4. When a sensitivity changes for a given change in market conditions, we can approximate the impact of that sensitivity by taking the average value of the sensitivity over the given change. (Recall that this was the method used in question 4 of the Risk Measurement section when estimating the effect of the delta and gamma together.)

a.	If volatility rises to 25%, what will be the approximate theoretical values of the 90 put and 100 call?	
b.	If the stock price rises to 107, what will be the new gamma values of the 100 call and 110 put?	
c.	If the stock price rises to 107, what will be the new delta values of the 100 call and the 110 put?	
d.	If the stock price rises to 107, what will be the approximate theoretical values of the 100 call and the 110 put?	

5. An option's elasticity is defined as the percent change in the option's value for a one percent change in the price of the underlying contract.

CALL VALUE	CALL ELASTICITY	PUT VALUE	PUT ELASTICITY
6.84	5.25	2.30	−2.90

a. If the price of the underlying contract rises from 54.80 to 56.34, what will be the new call and put values?

b. What are the delta values of the call and put?

c. How does an option's elasticity relate to its delta?

6. Option trades are sometimes "tied to" a specific underlying price. That is, a customer may want to trade an option and hedge it at an underlying price different than the current underlying price. Consider this situation:

    stock price = 73.50

    time to expiration = 2 months

    interest rate = 6.00%

    dividend = 0

    volatility = 25%

    theoretical value of the 75 call = 2.64

    delta of the 75 call = 48.0

    gamma of the 75 call = 5.3

a. What will be the option's approximate delta and theoretical value if the underlying stock price rises to 75.00?

b. Using the delta and gamma, in general what should be the new value of an option if the price of the underlying contract changes?

c. Suppose a customer wants to buy a 75 call tied to an underlying price of 75.00. (Perhaps the customer wants the option to be at-the-money.) If a market-maker takes the other side of this trade, what should be a fair price for the 75 call?

d. Using the theoretical value, delta, and gamma, what should be the "tied to" value of an option?

7. **A**—the price of the underlying stock rises

   B—volatility rises

   C—time passes

   D—interest rates rise

   E—the dividend is increased

   If the underlying contract is stock, for the questions below fill in all appropriate choices from the above list:

   a. Which of the above changes in market conditions will cause the *delta* of an at-the-money call to increase?

   b. Which of the above changes in market conditions will cause the *delta* of an out-of-the-money put to increase (become more negative)?

c. Which of the above changes in market conditions will cause the *gamma* of an at-the-money call to increase?

d. Which of the above changes in market conditions will cause the *gamma* of a deeply in-the-money put to increase?

e. Which of the above changes in market conditions will cause the *theta* of an at-the-money put to increase?

f. Which of the above changes in market conditions will cause the *vega* of an out-of-the-money call to increase?

8. Futures price = 149.65

time to August expiration = 8 weeks

annual volatility = 24.20%

You have the following position:

−32 August 140 puts

+30 August 160 calls

−15 August futures contracts

with the options having these risk sensitivities:

OPTION	DELTA	GAMMA	THETA	VEGA
August 140 put	−22.6	2.12	−.0381	.176
August 160 call	25.5	2.26	−.0407	.188

a. What is your total delta, gamma, theta, and vega position?

DELTA	GAMMA	THETA	VEGA

b. Considering only the delta, gamma, theta, and vega, how risky do you think this position is?

c. Is your conclusion in question b reasonable?

d. What will happen to your delta, gamma, and vega position (become positive or less negative, become negative or less positive, stay about the same) if the futures price rises while all other market conditions remain unchanged?

e. What will happen to your delta, gamma, and vega position (become positive or less negative, become negative or less positive, stay about the same) if the futures price falls while all other market conditions remain unchanged?

f. What will happen to your delta position (become positive or less negative, become negative or less positive, stay about the same) if volatility increases to 28% while all other market conditions remain unchanged?

g. What will happen to your delta position (become positive or less negative, become negative or less positive, stay about the same) if three weeks pass while all other market conditions remain unchanged?

h. Suppose the futures contract makes a very large downward move. What is your maximum downside delta?

i. Suppose the futures contract makes a very large upward move. What is your maximum upside delta?

j. Rank the order in which the following combination of market conditions will most help or hurt your position (1 = helps the most; 4 = hurts the most).

_____ the futures price falls slowly to 140 and implied volatility falls to 22.20%

_____ the futures price falls quickly to 140 and implied volatility rises to 26.20%

_____ the futures price rises slowly to 160 and implied volatility falls to 22.20%

_____ the futures price rises quickly to 160 and implied volatility rises to 26.20%

k. Suppose that under current market conditions the entire position has a theoretical P&L of zero. Using the grids below, and keeping in mind the current futures price (149.65) as well as the put and call exercise prices (140 and 160), try to draw an approximate graph of the position P&L (one graph), the position delta (a second graph), and position gamma (the third graph) with respect to the underlying futures price (futures prices on the x-axis; P&L, delta, or gamma on the y-axis). Then using the same grids (the x-axis is still the futures price), draw graphs of the P&L, delta, and gamma as implied volatility rises or falls. You don't need to be exact—the general shape of the graph and whether the values are positive or negative is sufficient.

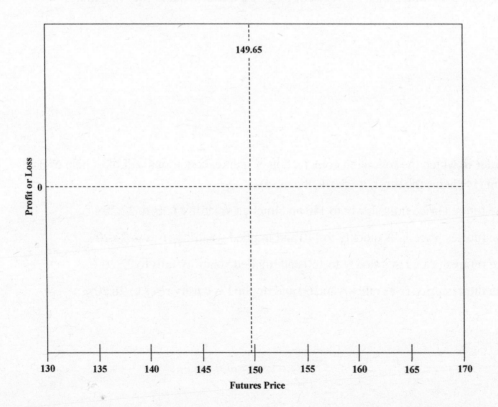

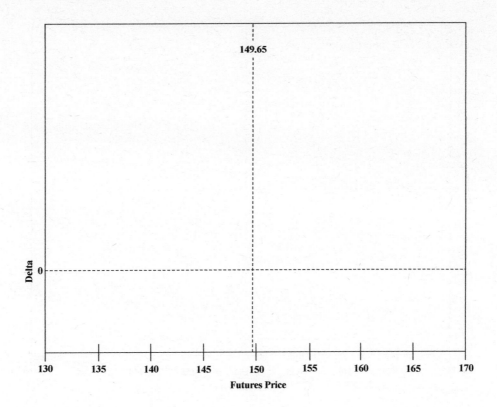

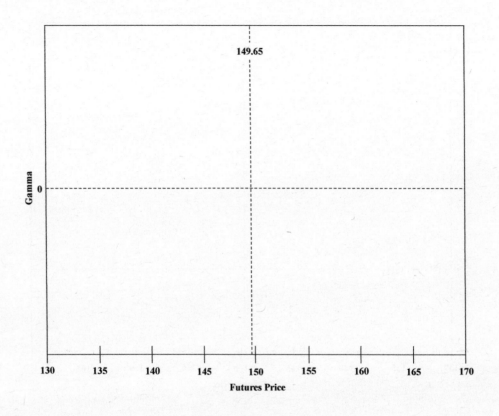

| CHAPTER 10 |

Spreading Strategies

Spreading strategies are among the most common strategies done in option markets. In a spreading strategy a trader will take a position in one contract or set of contracts, and an opposing position in a different contract or set of contracts. The opposing positions may be directional (delta), or they may be volatility (gamma or vega) positions.

1. Contracts are trading at the following prices:

CONTRACT A	CONTRACT B	CONTRACT C	CONTRACT D
46.75	70.30	81.80	59.15

What will be your credit (+) or debit (−) if you do each of the following?

a. buy 1 contract A and sell 1 contract C

b. buy 1 contract B and sell 1 contract D

c. buy 1 contract B and sell 2 contract A

d. buy 3 contract D and sell 2 contract C

e. buy 1 contract A, buy 1 contract D, and sell 1 contract C

f. buy 2 contract B, sell 1 contract C, and sell 1 contract D

2. In option trading a trader is said to have sold, or is short, a position if the entire trade results in a credit. A trader is said to have bought, or is long, a position if the entire trade results in a debit.

   For each spread position below, identify its name or type, and, where applicable, whether the spread is "long" or "short." Then, assuming that each position is approximately delta neutral, what is the initial sign (+ or –) of the gamma, theta, and vega?

		NAME OR TYPE	INITIAL GAMMA	INITIAL THETA	INITIAL VEGA
a.	+1 January 70 call +1 January 70 put				
b.	+1 February 65 call −1 March 65 call				
c.	+1February 70 put −3 February 60 puts				
d.	+1 March 55 call −2 March 60 calls +1 March 65 call				
e.	+1 March 65 call +1 March 75 put				
f.	+1 April 105 call −1 April 115 call −1 April 120 call				
g.	+1 June 100 put −1 April 100 put				
h.	+1 May 95 call −1 May 100 call −1 May 110 call +1 May 115 call				
i.	+2 April 120 calls −1 April 110 calls				

(continued on next page)

		NAME OR TYPE	INITIAL GAMMA	INITIAL THETA	INITIAL VEGA
j.	−1 June 105 put −1 June 120 call				
k.	−1 July 25 put +2 July 30 puts −1 July 35 put				
l.	+1 September 30 put +1 September 35 put −1 September 45 put				
m.	+1 July 35 put −1 August 35 put				
n.	+1 July 40 put +1 July 50 call				
o.	+1 August 40 call −2 August 45 calls				
p.	−1 October 30 put +1 October 35 put +1 October 40 put −1 October 45 put				
q.	+3 November 1850 puts −2 November 1900 puts				
r.	+1 December 2000 call −1 October 2000 call				
s.	−1 November 1900 call +2 November 2000 calls −1 November 2100 call				
t.	−1 December 2200 call −1 December 2200 put				

3. Option contracts are trading at the following prices with the given delta values:

	CALL PRICE	CALL DELTA	PUT PRICE	PUT DELTA
May 75	7.94	88	.43	−12
May 80	4.19	66	1.64	−34
May 85	1.77	38	4.18	−62
May 90	.59	17	7.97	−83
July 75	9.16	83	.96	−17
July 80	5.68	66	2.40	−34
July 85	3.17	46	4.81	−54
July 90	1.59	28	8.15	−72

Using the above table, what are the prices and delta values if you "buy" each of the following spreads?

	OPTION	PRICE	DELTA
a.	July 85 straddle		
b.	July/May 80 call calendar spread		
c.	May 75/85 1 × 2 call spread		
d.	July 80/85/90 put butterfly		
e.	July 75/90 strangle		
f.	May 80/85/90 put Christmas tree		

(continued on next page)

	OPTION	PRICE	DELTA
g.	July 75/85 1 × 3 put spread		
h.	May 75/80/85/90 call condor		
i.	July 80/85 "guts" strangle		

4. For each of the following groups of spreads you are given an underlying price, a directional outlook (bullish or bearish), and an opinion about implied volatility (unusually high or unusually low). Given this information, choose the best spread from among the four possible choices. Assume that all options expire at the same time.

	UNDERLYING PRICE	DIRECTIONAL OUTLOOK	IMPLIED VOLATILITY	SPREAD CHOICES
a.	90	bullish	unusually high	long a 95 put / short a 90 put long an 85 call / short a 90 call long a 90 put / short an 85 put long a 90 call / short an 85 call
b.	55	bearish	unusually low	long a 55 put / short a 50 put long a 55 put / short a 60 put long a 50 call / short a 55 call long a 60 call / short a 55 call
c.	127	bearish	unusually high	long a 135 put / short a 140 put long a 120 call / short a 130 call long a 115 put / short a 125 put long a 135 call / short a 125 call
d.	2485	bullish	unusually low	long a 2500 call / short a 2300 call long a 2500 call / short a 2700 call long a 2500 put / short a 2300 put long a 2300 put / short a 2500 put

5. Below are several different stock option positions with some suggested changes in market conditions. If the underlying stock is currently trading at 80, for each change in market conditions, is the position making money (+), losing money (–), or staying about the same (0)? Assume that all options are European, and that dividends are paid quarterly. For ratio spreads (the number of long and short market contracts are unequal), assume that the spread is approximately delta neutral.

a.

	THE STOCK PRICE RISES SHARPLY	TIME PASSES WITH NO MOVEMENT	IMPLIED VOLATILITY RISES
1 March 80 call −1 March 90 call			

b.

	THE STOCK PRICE RISES SHARPLY	TIME PASSES WITH NO MOVEMENT	IMPLIED VOLATILITY RISES
+2 March 75 puts −1 March 80 put			

c.

	INTEREST RATES RISE SHARPLY	TIME PASSES WITH NO MOVEMENT	IMPLIED VOLATILITY FALLS
+1 March 80 put −1 June 80 put			

d.

	THE STOCK PRICE FALLS SHARPLY	TIME PASSES WITH VOLATILITY FALLS	IMPLIED NO MOVEMENT
+1 June 75 put −2 June 80 puts +1 June 85 put			

e.

	THE STOCK PRICE RISES SHARPLY	TIME PASSES WITH NO MOVEMENT	IMPLIED VOLATILITY RISE
+1 March 80 call +1 March 80 put			

f.

	THE STOCK PRICE RISES SHARPLY	THE DIVIDEND IS REDUCED	IMPLIED VOLATILITY FALLS
−1 March 80 call +1 June 80 call			

g.

	THE STOCK PRICE FALLS SHARPLY	TIME PASSES WITH NO MOVEMENT	IMPLIED VOLATILITY FALLS
−3 June 85 calls +1 June 75 call			

h.

	INTEREST RATES FALL SHARPLY	THE DIVIDEND IS INCREASED	IMPLIED VOLATILITY FALLS
−1 March 80 put +1 June 80 put			

6. With the underlying contract trading close to 50, in each group of spreading strategies choose both the strategy that will have the highest price and the strategy that will have the lowest price in the marketplace. Assume that there are no interest or dividend considerations, and that April options expire before June options.

a. +1 April 40 call / –1 April 45 call

+1 April 45 call / –1 April 50 call

+1 April 50 call / –1 April 55 call

+1 April 55 call / –1 April 60 call

b. +1 April 35 put / –1 April 45 put

+1 April 40 put / –1 April 45 put

+1 April 40 put / –1 April 50 put

+1 April 45 put / –1 April 55 put

c. +1 June 45 call / –1 June 50 call

+1 June 50 call / –1 June 55 call

+1 April 45 call / –1 April 50 call

+1 April 50 call / –1 April 55 call

d. +1 April 55 call / +1 April 55 put

+1 April 60 call / +1 April 60 put

+1 April 50 call / +1 April 50 put

+1 April 45 call / +1 April 45 put

e. +1 April 50 call / +1 April 50 put

   +1 June 50 call / +1 June 50 put

   +1 April 55 call / +1 April 55 put

   +1 June 55 call / +1 June 55 put

f. +1 April 45 call / –2 April 50 calls / +1 April 55 call

   +1 April 40 put / –2 April 50 puts / +1 April 60 put

   +1 April 40 call / –2 April 45 calls / +1 April 50 call

   +1 April 45 put / –2 April 50 puts / +1 April 55 put

g. +1 April 40 call / –2 April 45 calls / +1 April 50 call

   +1 June 50 put / –2 June 55 puts / +1 June 60 put

   +1 April 40 put / –2 April 50 puts / +1 April 60 put

   +1 June 40 call / –2 June 50 calls / +1 June 60 call

h. +1 June 50 call / –1 April 50 call

   +1 June 55 call / –1 April 55 call

   +1 June 45 put / –1 April 45 put

   +1 June 40 put / –1 April 40 put

CHAPTER 11

Synthetic Equivalents

For any contract, there is a synthetic equivalent that has essentially (although perhaps not identically) the same characteristics as the actual contract. This also means that almost any strategy can be done using a synthetic equivalent.

There are six basic synthetic equivalents:

$$\text{long underlying} \approx \text{long call} + \text{short put}$$
$$\text{short underlying} \approx \text{short call} + \text{long put}$$

$$\text{long call} \approx \text{long put} + \text{long underlying}$$
$$\text{short call} \approx \text{short put} + \text{short underlying}$$

$$\text{long put} \approx \text{long call} + \text{short underlying}$$
$$\text{short put} \approx \text{short call} + \text{long underlying}$$

In a synthetic equivalent including a call and put, the options are assumed to have the same exercise price and expiration date.

1. For each combination of contracts below, from the given choices select the equivalent strategy.

a.	+1 January 60 call −1 January 60 put	long straddle long an underlying contract short straddle none of the above
b.	−1 February 1,000 put −1 underlying contract	+1 February 1000 call long an underlying contract −1 February 1000 call none of the above
c.	+1 March 150 call +1 March 150 put	long straddle short an underlying contract long an underlying contract none of the above
d.	−1 April 600 call −1 underlying contract	+1 April 600 put long an underlying contract −1 April 600 put none of the above
e.	−1 May 75 call +1 underlying contract	+1 May 75 put short an underlying contract −1 May 75 put none of the above
f.	−2 June 5,000 puts −1 underlying contract	+1 June 5000 call short straddle −1 June 5000 put none of the above
g.	+1 July 40 call +1 underlying contract	−1 July 40 put +1 July 40 put short an underlying contract none of the above

(continued on next page)

h.	+1 August 1500 call −1 underlying contract	long an underlying contract +1 August 1500 put −1 August 1500 call none of the above
i.	+1 September 200 put +1 underlying	short an underlying contract +1 September 200 call −1 September 200 put none of the above
j.	+1 October 80 put −1 underlying contract	+1 October 80 call −1 October 80 put −1 October 80 call none of the above
k.	−1 November 125 call +1 November 125 put	long straddle short an underlying contract short straddle none of the above
l.	+2 December 55 calls −1 underlying contract	long straddle long an underlying contract +2 December 55 puts none of the above
m.	+1 March 60 put −1 March 65 put −1 March 70 call +1 March 75 call	long butterfly short condor long condor none of the above
n.	−1 September 225 put +1 September 250 put +1 September 250 call −1 September 275 call	long butterfly short butterfly short condor none of the above

2. Spreads that are done using synthetic equivalents are sometimes preceded with the term *iron*. The most common of these are iron butterflies and iron condors.

   a. Using synthetic equivalents, show that the following long iron butterfly, composed of a long straddle and short strangle, is equivalent to a traditional short butterfly.

   −1 October 80 put

   +1 October 85 put

   +1 October 85 call

   −1 October 90 call

   b. Using synthetic equivalents, show that the following short iron condor, composed of a long strangle and short strangle or, alternatively, a short put spread and short call spread, is equivalent to a traditional long condor.

   +1 October 75 put

   −1 October 80 put

   −1 October 85 call

   +1 October 90 call

3. Using synthetic equivalents, show that the following position is equivalent to a 1 × 2 call ratio spread:

> −16 underlying contracts
>
> −9 May 45 calls
>
> −11 May 45 puts
>
> +26 May 50 calls
>
> +14 May 50 puts
>
> +19 May 55 calls
>
> −19 May 55 puts

4. Using synthetic equivalents, show that the following position is equivalent to a short butterfly:

> −8 underlying contracts
>
> −21 July 70 calls
>
> +56 July 70 puts
>
> +30 July 80 calls
>
> +40 July 80 puts
>
> +43 July 90 calls
>
> −8 July 90 puts

| CHAPTER 12 |

Synthetic Pricing and Arbitrage

For the questions in this section, assume that all options are European (no possibility of early exercise). All calculations should be made using simple interest, rather than compound or continuous interest. Assume that a year is made up of 365 days, 52 weeks, or 12 months. Answers should be expressed to the nearest .01 for contract prices, to the nearest .01% for interest rates, and to the nearest whole number for days to expiration.

Basic put-call parity:

call price – put price = (forward price – exercise price) / (1 + interest rate × time)

1. Options on futures; futures-type settlement (an effective interest rate of zero)

    a. Fill in the missing values for options on a futures contract.

    Futures price = 61.75

EXERCISE PRICE	45	50	55	60	65	70	75	80
call price		11.90		4.05		.70		.10
put price	.05		.75		5.10		13.50	

b. For each option below, fill in the missing value.

FUTURES PRICE	EXERCISE PRICE	CALL PRICE	PUT PRICE
152.65	140	15.80	
	475	6.99	20.48
80.87		4.48	3.61
26.77	25		.22
3,352.00 –	3,500	1.45	
760.85		4.65	43.80
1,441.20	1,500		71.70
	55	1.56	2.45

c.

	BID PRICE	OFFER PRICE
June future	410.15	410.35
June 400 call	14.90	15.15
June 400 put	4.85	5.00

Suppose that there are no transaction costs, but you will always have to buy at the offer price and sell at the bid price. From the bid and offer prices above, what is the best way to . . .

i. buy a June futures contract?

ii. sell the June 400 call?

iii. sell the June 400 put?

2. Options on futures; stock-type settlement

    a. Fill in the missing values for options on a futures contract.

        Futures price = 1,245.00

        Time to expiration = 4 months

        Interest rate = 6.00%

EXERCISE PRICE	1,050	1,100	1,150	1,200	1,250	1,300	1,350	1,400
call price	192.45		104.85		42.65		12.30	
put price		4.40		25.55		77.85		157.70

    b. For each option below, fill in the missing value.

FUTURES PRICE	EXERCISE PRICE	TIME TO EXPIRATION (DAYS)	INTEREST RATE	CALL PRICE	PUT PRICE
	300	23	3.72%	.20	41.33
114.47	120	74		2.28	7.78
47.62	45	160	7.65%		1.98
2,264.75	2,200		1.75%	149.04	84.93
858.40	900	91	4.00%	17.80	

c. You have the following position:

+1 June 80 call

–1 June 80 put

–1 futures contract

If interest rates are 8.00%, using the whole number format for the delta, to the nearest .1 delta what is your total delta position if there are . . .

i. 12 months to expiration?

ii. 9 months to expiration?

iii. 6 months to expiration?

iv. 3 months to expiration?

3. Options on stock

Rather than use the original form for put-call parity,

call price − put price = (forward price − exercise price) / (1 + interest rate × time)

stock option traders sometimes use this approximation in order to simplify the arithmetic:

call price − put price = stock price − exercise price + (exercise price × interest × time) − dividends

In the following questions you may use either the full form or the approximation. The approximation may result in answers slightly different than those given in the answer section.

a. Ignoring interest on dividends, fill in the missing values for options on stock.

Stock price = 150.10

Time to expiration = 2 months

Interest rate = 3.00%

Expected dividends = .85

EXERCISE PRICE	130	135	140	145	150	155	160	165
call price		16.30		9.25		4.45		1.85
put price	.70		2.55		6.55		12.90	

b. For each option below, fill in the missing value.

STOCK PRICE	EXERCISE PRICE	TIME TO EXPIRATION (DAYS)	INTEREST RATE	EXPECTED DIVIDENDS	CALL PRICE	PUT PRICE
260.03	270	34	5.69%	2.00		14.04
23.97	25	137	3.32%		1.31	2.20
446.75	450	96		1.75	17.30	17.30
86.05	80	73	4.50%	.62	8.27	
	125	64	8.00%	.95	5.72	3.93
59.15	50		2.71%	0	10.70	.70

c. You have the following position:

−1 March 80 call

+1 March 80 put

+1 stock contract

Which of the following changes in market conditions will help your position (+), which will hurt your position (−), and which will have no effect (0)?

Assume that the dividend will be paid prior to March expiration.

i. the stock price rises _____

ii. the dividend is increased _____

     iii. implied volatility rises _____

     iv. the stock price falls _____

     v. interest rates rise _____

     vi. implied volatility falls _____

     vii. the dividend is reduced _____

     viii. interest rates fall _____

4. Boxes

A box consists of buying a synthetic underlying at one exercise price and selling a synthetic underlying at a different exercise price, where all options expire at the same time.

box value = (higher exercise price − lower exercise price) / (1 + interest rate × time)

a. If all options are subject to stock-type settlement, fill in the missing values below.

LOWER EXERCISE PRICE	HIGHER EXERCISE PRICE	TIME TO EXPIRATION (DAYS)	INTEREST RATE	BOX VALUE
80	90	78	3.30%	
125	150	35	5.00%	
320	360	143	1.93%	
40	45	283		4.72
1,100	1,300		2.11%	196.49

b. A box can also be thought of as the combination of a call spread and a put spread:

box value = call spread value + put spread value

If all options are subject to stock-type settlement, fill in the missing values below.

LOWER EXERCISE PRICE	HIGHER EXERCISE PRICE	TIME TO EXPIRATION (DAYS)	INTEREST RATE	CALL SPREAD	PUT SPREAD
65	80	54	2.71%	10.22	
20	25	122	8.60%		2.00
2,500	2,600	256		80.50	16.50
700	775		1.91%	33.28	41.02

5. Rolls

A roll in the stock option market consists of buying a synthetic underlying in one expiration month and selling a synthetic underlying in a different expiration month, where all options have the same exercise price.

roll value = exercise price / (1 + interest rate × time to short-term expiration)

− exercise price / (1 + interest rate × time to long-term expiration)

− expected dividends between expirations

Rather than use the full form for the roll, stock option traders sometimes use this approximation:

roll value = exercise price × time between expirations × interest rate − expected dividends between expirations

In the following questions you may use either the full form or the approximation. The approximation may result in answers slightly different than those given in the answer section.

a. Ignoring interest on dividends, fill in the missing values below for options on stock. Assume the same interest rate applies to all expirations.

EXERCISE PRICE	TIME TO SHORT-TERM EXPIRATION (DAYS)	TIME TO LONG-TERM EXPIRATION (DAYS)	INTEREST RATE	DIVIDENDS BETWEEN EXPIRATIONS	ROLL VALUE
70	35	63	3.01%	0	
125	15	78	7.75%	.32	
35	44	72	2.63%		−.11
100	65	156	5.64%		.84

b. A roll can also be thought of as the difference between two calendar spreads:

roll value = call calendar spread value − put calendar spread value

Ignoring interest on dividends, fill in the missing values below for options on stock. Assume the same interest rate applies to all expirations.

EXERCISE PRICE	TIME TO SHORT-TERM EXPIRATION (DAYS)	TIME TO LONG-TERM EXPIRATION (DAYS)	INTEREST RATE	DIVIDENDS BETWEEN EXPIRATIONS	CALL CALENDAR SPREAD	PUT CALENDAR SPREAD
200	21	49	1.96%	.15	2.00	
45	8	43	8.21%	.10		1.25
90	65	93	3.83%		2.55	2.85
115	30	121	6.08%		3.45	2.40

6. From the given prices, try to fill in the missing prices for the stock options below. Assume that all options are European and fairly priced, and that the stock pays no dividend.

time to expiration = 73 days

	120	130	140	150	160	170
calls		19.92	12.37		3.35	1.46
puts	.29	1.23		7.99	14.42	

7. The February 110 / 120 / 130 butterfly is trading at a price of 3.25. If interest rates are zero, and the February 120 straddle is trading for 9.50, what should be the price of the February 110 / 130 strangle?

8. The August 40 / 45 call spread is trading for 4.00. If interest rates are zero, and the August 40 / 45 / 55 / 60 iron condor is trading for 2.00, what should be the price of the August 50 / 55 call spread?

CHAPTER 13

Early Exercise of American Options

All options have a lower arbitrage boundary. If the option is trading at a price below this lower arbitrage boundary, and there are no transaction costs, then a trader can be certain of a profit by buying the option and hedging the option position against the underlying contract.

The lower arbitrage boundary for European options:

call: maximum [forward price – exercise price) / (1 + interest rate × time),0]

put: maximum [exercise price – forward price) / (1 + interest rate × time),0]

The lower arbitrage boundary for American options:

maximum [European lower arbitrage boundary, intrinsic value]

In questions 1 and 2, what are the lower arbitrage boundaries for the given options if they are both European and American? In other words, if there are no transaction costs, what is the lowest price at which the option can trade such that there is no arbitrage profit available? All calculations should be made using simple, rather than compound or continuous, interest. A year consists of 12 months, 52 weeks, or 365 days. Answers should be expressed to the nearest .01.

1. Options on futures; stock-type settlement

OPTION	FUTURES PRICE	TIME TO EXPIRATION	INTEREST RATE	LOWER ARBITRAGE BOUNDARY	
				EUROPEAN	AMERICAN
40 put	37.66	134 days	3.95%		
90 call	94.50	4 months	6.00%		
150 call	143.80	7 weeks	4.10%		
500 put	425.00	83 days	5.25%		
1200 put	1,255.00	1 month	2.37%		
3000 call	3,463.00	44 weeks	1.20%		

2. **a.** Options on stock. You can ignore interest on dividends. Assume that there are no restrictions on the short sale of stock, and that the same interest rate applies to all transactions.

| | | | | | | LOWER ARBITRAGE BOUNDARY | | | |
| | | | | | | EUROPEAN | | AMERICAN | |
EXERCISE PRICE	STOCK PRICE	TIME TO EXPIRATION	INTEREST RATE	EXPECTED DIVIDEND	FORWARD PRICE	CALL	PUT	CALL	PUT
25	24.75	30 weeks	7.60%	.0					
65	68.75	2 months	2.30%	.50					
90	88.90	180 days	4.66%	.33					
130	116.50	5 weeks	6.80%	.45					
500	510.80	1 month	8.74%	5.80					
550	552.15	8 weeks	5.25%	8.30					
1,350	1,355.00	27 days	1.75%	9.25					
2,500	2,231.40	102 days	3.13%	1.56					

b. From your answers above, do you think the following statements are true or false?

  i. If the lower arbitrage boundary for a European stock option call is a positive value, the lower arbitrage boundary for a European stock option put with the same exercise price and expiration date must be zero.

  ii. If the lower arbitrage boundary for an American stock option call is a positive value, the lower arbitrage boundary for an American stock option put with the same exercise price and expiration date must be zero.

c. Under what conditions will the lower arbitrage boundaries for a European call and put with the same exercise price and expiration date both be zero?

d. Using your answers to question 2a above, suppose you are able to buy the 90 put for .85.

   i. If the option is American, what can you do to ensure a profit?

   ii. If you take the appropriate action, what will be your total profit?

e. Using your answers to question 2a above, suppose you are able to buy the 25 call for .60.

   i. If the option is European, what can you do to ensure a profit?

If you take the appropriate action, what will be your total profit at expiration if . . .

ii. the stock price at expiration is 30?

iii. the stock price at expiration is 20?

3. Options on futures

For a futures option to be an early exercise candidate, the option must be subject to stock-type settlement. In addition, the following must also hold true over the entire life of the option, as well as over the next day:

interest earned through early exercise > volatility value.

where

the interest that can be earned is the interest on the option's intrinsic value.

the volatility value over the life of the option is approximately equal to the price of the companion out-of-the-money option.

the volatility value over the next day is approximately equal to the theta of the companion out-of-the-money option.

Futures price = 1,325.00

time to March expiration = 26 days

interest rate = 6.00%

You own a March 1200 call that can be exercised early. All options are subject to stock-type settlement.

a. What must be the price of the March 1200 put in order for the March 1200 call to be an early exercise candidate? Why?

b. What must be the daily theta of the March 1200 put for you to want to exercise the March 1200 call right now?

4. Call options on stock

For a stock option call to be an early exercise candidate, the following must hold true over the entire life of the option, as well as over the next day:

$$dividend > interest\ cost + volatility\ value$$

where

the interest cost is equal to exercise price × interest rate × time.

the volatility value over the life of the option is approximately equal to the price of the companion out-of-the-money option. The volatility value over the next day is approximately equal to the theta of the companion out-of-the-money option.

stock price = 60.00

time to May expiration = 35 days

interest rate = 4.00%

dividend = .50, payable in 15 days

You own a May 50 call that can be exercised early.

a. Suppose there are only two choices, exercise now or hold the option to expiration. If the May 50 put is trading at a price of .20, which choice is best? Why?

b. If this is a true American call, allowing for exercise at any time prior to expiration, when will you optimally decide whether to exercise the option?

c. If the stock price remains unchanged at 60, on the day you must optimally decide whether to exercise the option, at what price must the May 50 put be trading in order for you to exercise the May 50 call?

d. If you decide to exercise the May 50 call but want the same protective characteristics offered by the May 50 call, what should you do?

e. If you take the appropriate action in question 4d, how much better off will you be with your new position than if you had not exercised the May 50 call?

5. Put options on stock

In the following questions ignore any short stock considerations.

For a stock option put to be an early exercise candidate, the following must hold true over the entire life of the option, as well as over the next day:

interest earned > dividend + volatility value

where

the interest earned is equal to exercise price × interest rate × time.

the volatility value over the life of the option is approximately equal to the price of the companion out-of-the-money option. The volatility value over the next day is approximately equal to the theta of the companion out-of-the-money option.

The "blackout period" for a stock option put is the period prior to the payment of the dividend when it is not possible to earn enough interest through early exercise to offset the loss of the dividend.

stock price = 82.50

time to July expiration = 54 days

interest rate = 5.00%

dividend = .25

You own a July 95 put that can be exercised early.

a. What is the blackout period, in days, for this option? (Within what number of days prior to the dividend payment would you never consider exercising the July 95 put?)

b. If there are 37 days until the dividend payment, at what price must the July 95 call be trading for you to consider immediate early exercise of the July 95 put?

c. In addition to the price of the July 95 call, what must be the daily theta of the July 95 call for immediate exercise of the July 95 put to be optimal?

d. If the daily theta of the July 95 call is .015 (in absolute value), would you exercise the July 95 put now?

e. If there are 10 days until the dividend payment date, at what price must the July 95 call be trading for you to want to immediately exercise the July 95 put?

6. Assuming that each of the stock options below is in-the-money, which of the options should be exercised immediately?

OPTION	TIME TO EXPIRATION	INTEREST RATE	EXPECTED DIVIDEND	TIME TO DIVIDEND	COMPANION OPTION PRICE	THETA
80 call	24 days	4.50%	.48	6 days	.10	−.0107
45 put	32 days	6.15%	.15	14 days	.05	−.0045
100 call	51 days	2.33%	.59	1 day	.15	−.0087
150 put	64 days	67.49%	0	—	.75	−.0239
125 call	39 days	5.62%	1.00	1 day	.31	−.0165
275 put	41 days	3.78%	0	—	.66	−.0362

a. 80 call?

b. 45 put?

c. 100 call?

d. 150 put?

e. 125 call?

f. 275 put?

7. A stock that is currently trading at a price of 61.00 is expected to pay a dividend of .75 approximately 10 weeks prior to option expiration. If interest rates are 8.00% what can you say about the likelihood of the 50 call being exercised early?

8. a. You are considering early exercise of an option. Would you be more likely to exercise the option early if implied volatility rises, implied volatility remains unchanged, or implied volatility falls?

    b. Assume that you will earn less interest on a short stock position than the normal prevailing interest rate.

        i. You are considering early exercise of a stock option call. Would you be more likely to exercise the call early if you currently are long stock, have no stock position, or are short stock?

        ii. You are considering early exercise of a stock option put. Would you be more likely to exercise the put early if you currently are long stock, have no stock position, or are short stock?

9. In this question, ignore any short stock considerations.

Consider a June 150 /175 box under the following conditions:

time to June expiration = 38 days

interest rate = 7.50%

dividend = 1.15

time to dividend payment = 16 days

a. What should be the minimum value of the box? Under what market conditions is this likely to occur?

b. What should be the value of the box if both the June 150 call and the June 175 call should optimally be exercised early? Under what conditions is this likely to occur?

c. What should be the value of the box if both the June 150 put and the June 175 put should optimally be exercised early?

d. What should be the value of the box if only the June 150 call should optimally be exercised early?

e. What should be the value of the box if only the June 175 put should optimally be exercised early?

f. What should be the value of the box if both the June 150 call and the June 175 put should optimally be exercised early? Under what market conditions is this likely to occur?

CHAPTER 14

The Black-Scholes Model

For the questions in this section, you will probably need to use a computer spreadsheet.

For the formulas in this section, if:

S = the spot price or underlying price

X = the exercise price

t = the time to expiration in years

r = the annual interest rate

σ = the annualized volatility

$e^x = \exp(x)$ = the exponential function

$\ln$ = the natural logarithm

$n(x)$ = the standard normal distribution function

$N(x)$ = the cumulative normal distribution function

(The standard normal distribution and cumulative normal distribution functions are commonly included in most spreadsheets.)

then the value of a European call, C, and a European put, P, are given by

$$C = Se^{(b-r)t}N(d_1) - Xe^{-rt}N(d_2) \qquad\qquad P = Xe^{-rt}N(-d_2) - Se^{(b-r)t}N(-d_1)$$

$$\text{where } d_1 = [\ln(S/X) + (b + \sigma^2/2)t] / \sigma\sqrt{t} \qquad d_2 = [\ln(S/X) + (b - \sigma^2/2)t] / \sigma\sqrt{t} = d_1 - \sigma\sqrt{t}$$

The common variations on the original Black-Scholes model are determined by the value of b.

$b = r$ The Black-Scholes model for options on stock

$b = r = 0$ The Black-Scholes model for options on futures where the options are subject to futures-type settlement

$b = 0$ The Black-Scholes model (sometimes referred to as the Black model) for options on futures where the options are subject to stock-type settlement.

Black-Scholes Sensitivities

	CALLS		PUTS		
Delta (Δ)	$e^{(b-r)t}N(d_1)$		$e^{(b-r)t}[N(d_1) - 1]$		
Gamma (Γ)	$e^{(b-r)t}N(d_1)/So\sqrt{t}$				same for calls and puts
Theta (Θ)*	$-[Se^{(b-r)t}n(d_1)\sigma]/2\sqrt{t} - (b-r)Se^{(b-r)t}N(d_1) - rXe^{-rt}N(d_2)$		$-[Se^{(b-r)t}n(d_1)\sigma]/2\sqrt{t} + (b-r)Se^{(b-r)t}N(-d_1) + rXe^{-rt}N(-d_2)$		
Vega**	$Se^{(b-r)t}n(d_1)\sqrt{t}$				same for calls and puts
Rho**	$-tC$	if $b=0$	$-tP$	if $b=0$	
	$tXe^{-rt}N(d_2)$	if $b \ne 0$	$-tXe^{-rt}N(-d_2)$	if $b \ne 0$	

*The theta formula represents the sensitivity of the option to the passage of one full year. To express the theta in the more common form of daily decay, the theta must be divided by 365, the number of days in a year.
**The vega and rho formulas represent the sensitivity of the option to a one full point (100%) change in volatility or interest rates. To express the vega and rho in the more common form of the sensitivity to one percentage point (1%) change in volatility or interest rates, the vega and rho must be divided by 100.

1. stock price (S) = 71.60

exercise price (X) = 75

time to expiration (t) = 86 days

interest rate (r) = 5.45%

volatility (σ) = 29.30%

dividend = 0

a. Using the above inputs, calculate, step-by-step, the Black-Scholes theoretical value and delta for a stock option call.

S/X

$\ln(S/X)$

t (in years)

$\sqrt{t}$

$\sigma\sqrt{t}$

rt

e^{-rt}

d_1

d_2

$N(d_1)$

$N(d_2)$

call value

call delta

b. What is the probability the 75 call will finish in-the-money?

2. futures price (*S*) = 1,200

exercise price (*X*) = 1,200

time to expiration (*t*) = 149 days

interest rate (*r*) = 3.60%

volatility (*σ*) = 18.85%

a. Using the above inputs, calculate, step-by-step, the theoretical value, delta, gamma, theta (per day), vega (per one percentage point), and rho (per one percentage point) for a futures option put that is subject to stock-type settlement.

F/X

$\ln(F/X)$

t (in years)

$\sqrt{t}$

$\sigma\sqrt{t}$

rt

e^{-rt}

d_1

d_2

$N(d_1)$

$N(d_2)$

$N(-d_1)$

$N(-d_2)$

$n(d_1)$

put value

put delta

put gamma

put theta

put vega

put rho

b. The "40% rule" states that the expected value of an option whose exercise price is exactly equal to the forward price of the underlying contract (the option is "at-the-forward") is approximately equal to 40% of a one standard deviation price change at expiration. The theoretical value is the present value of the expected value.

Using the "40% rule," what is your estimated value for the 1200 put? How does this compare to your calculated value in question 2a?

| CHAPTER 15 |

Binomial Pricing

At any point along a binomial tree the price of underlying contract, i, can move up to Su or down to Sd. In a risk-neutral market the average price of Su and Sd must be equal to the forward price. For a non–dividend paying stock, the probability of an up move, p, must be:

$$[(1 + rt) - d] / (u - d)$$

and the probability of a down move must be:

$$1 - p$$

If the underlying price moves up to Su or down to Sd, the terminal values of a call (C_u or C_d) or put (P_u or P_d) are:

$$\text{call value} = \text{maximum } [S - X, 0]$$
$$\text{put value} = \text{maximum } [X - S, 0]$$

The expected values for a call or put are:

$$\text{call expected value} = pC_u + (1 - p)C_d$$
$$\text{put expected value} = pP_u + (1 - p)P_d$$

The theoretical value is the present value of the expected value (the expected value discounted by interest).

The delta values for a call and put in a binomial tree are:

$$\Delta_c = (C_u - C_d) / (Su - Sd)$$
$$\Delta_p = (P_u - P_d) / (Su - Sd)$$

1. stock price $(S) = 82.50$

time to expiration $(t) = 2$ months

interest rate $(r) = 6\%$

u (an upward move) $= 1.15$

d (a downward move) $= .90$

a. What are the risk-neutral probabilities of an upward move, p, and a downward move, $1 - p$?

b. What are the values of S for both an upward move (Su) and downward move (Sd)?

c. What are the values of the 80 call and 80 put at both Su and Sd?

d. What are the theoretical values of the 80 call and 80 put?

e. Show that put-call parity is maintained for the 80 call and 80 put.

f. What are the delta values of the 80 call (Δ_c) and 80 put (Δ_p)?

g. Show that if you buy the 80 call at its theoretical value and correctly hedge the position, regardless of whether the stock moves up to *Su* or down to *Sd*, you will just break even.

h. Show that if you buy the 80 put at a price .25 less than its theoretical value and correctly hedge the position, regardless of whether the stock moves up to Su or down to Sd, you will always show a profit of .25.

i. An American option can never be worth less than intrinsic value. Therefore the value of an American option at any point along a binomial tree must be maximum [European value, intrinsic value].

Suppose this stock is expected to pay a dividend of 1.50 over the next two months. What is the value of the 70 call if it is both European and American? If you own the 70 call and it is American, what action should you take?

j. Suppose we are in a hyperinflationary market where interest rates are 100% annually. Using the same u (1.15) and d (.90), what are the new values of p and $1 - p$? What can you conclude from the new probabilities?

2. In this section, depending on whether the calculations are done with a spreadsheet or by hand, there may be slight rounding errors.

> time to expiration = 30 weeks (1 week = 1/52 year)
>
> annual interest rates = 4%
>
> annual volatility = 27%
>
> stock index price = 1,278.00
>
> expected dividends = 0

a. In a 3-period binomial tree, what is the discounting factor (using simple interest) over each period in the tree?

b. If $u = e^{\sigma x \sqrt{t}}$ and $d = 1/u = e^{-\sigma x \sqrt{t}}$, in a 3-period binomial tree what are the values of u (an upward move), d (a downward move), and the risk neutral probabilities of an upward move (p) and downward move ($1 - p$)?

c. What are the terminal values for the index at the end of the three periods?

d. Using the probabilities, p and $1 - p$, what is the probability of reaching each terminal price?

e. How many different paths lead from the initial price of 1,278 ($S_{0,0}$) to each terminal price?

f. What are the values of the 1300 put at each terminal price?

g. Using the terminal values for the 1300 put, the number of paths to each terminal price, the values of p and $1 - p$, and the discount factor over each period, calculate the initial (theoretical) value of the European 1300 put in a 3-period binomial tree.

h. Insert the index prices at each branch in the 3-period binomial tree below.

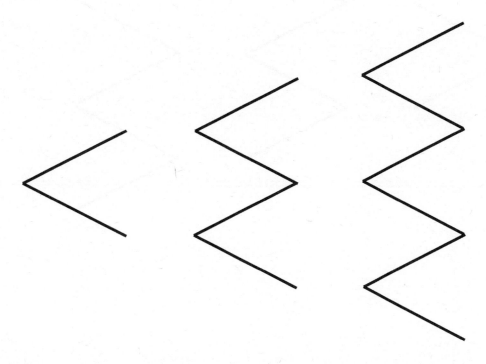

i. Using the terminal prices in the above tree, and using the values of p and $1 - p$, insert the European values for the 1300 put at each branch in the binomial tree. (Remember to discount the expected value by interest in order to obtain the present value at each branch.)

j. The gamma values for either a call or put in a binomial tree are:

$$\Gamma = (\Delta_u - \Delta_d) / (Su - Sd)$$

Using the values in the above tree, where possible, insert the delta and gamma at each branch in the binomial tree.

k. What is the approximate weekly theta for the European 1300 put?

3. Suppose the 1300 put in question 2 is an American option.

   a. Using the underlying prices from your binomial tree in question 2h, fill in the theoretical value, delta, and gamma for the 1300 put at each branch on the 3-period binomial tree below.

   b. What is the approximate weekly theta for the American 1300 put?

CHAPTER 16

Hedging Strategies

1. Besides trading a futures contract, for someone trying to protect an underlying position, the two most common, and simplest, hedging strategies using options are:

   buy a protective option

   sell a covered option

   You are currently long stock on which both futures and options are available.

   a. Which of the following strategies will offset at least some of your risk?

   _____ buy a futures contract

   _____ sell a futures contract

   _____ buy a call

   _____ sell a call

   _____ buy a put

   _____ sell a put

   b. For each of your choices in part a, choose the characteristics from the list below that go with each hedging strategy

   i. limited profit potential

   ii. limited risk

   iii. unlimited profit potential

    iv. unlimited risk

    v. no profit potential

    vi. no risk

    vii. results in a credit

    viii. results in a debit

c. For each of your choices in part b, which strategies should you prefer if:

    i. implied volatility is high (all options seem expensive)?

    ii. implied volatility is low (all options seem cheap)?

2. In addition to common hedging strategies, an underlying position can also be hedged with a more complex strategy. Any option position with a negative delta can be used to hedge a long underlying position, and any option position with a positive delta can be used to hedge a short underlying position. By choosing appropriate exercise prices, almost all common spreading strategies can be done in such a way as to create a positive or negative delta position. However, unlike the strategies in question 1, which always maintain the same sign for the delta, the delta for a complex strategy may invert, going from positive to negative, or negative to positive, as market conditions change. When this occurs, the spread may no longer act as a hedge, and may, in fact, add to the risk.

You are currently long stock, with the stock trading at a price close to 50.

a. Which of the following strategies will offset at least some of your risk? (That is, which strategies have a negative delta?)

    _____ buy a 40 call calendar spread

    _____ buy a 40 put calendar spread

_____ sell a 40 call calendar spread

_____ sell a 40 put calendar spread

_____ buy a 60 call calendar spread

_____ buy a 60 put calendar spread

_____ sell a 60 call calendar spread

_____ sell a 60 put calendar spread

_____ buy a 60 straddle

_____ sell a 60 straddle

_____ buy a 40 straddle

_____ sell a 40 straddle

_____ buy a 45 / 50 call spread

_____ sell a 45 / 50 call spread

_____ buy a 45 / 50 put spread

_____ sell a 45 / 50 put spread

_____ buy a 50 / 55 call spread

_____ sell a 50 / 55 call spread

_____ buy a 50 / 55 put spread

_____ sell a 50 / 55 put spread

b. For each of your choices in part a, choose the characteristics from the list below that go with each hedging strategy.

    i. limited profit potential

    ii. limited risk

    iii. unlimited profit potential

    iv. unlimited risk

    v. results in a credit

    vi. results in a debit

c. For each of your choices in part a, which strategies would you prefer if implied volatility is high (all options seem expensive)?

3. A *collar* consists of simultaneously buying a protective option and selling a covered option. A long collar is used to hedge a long underlying position; a short collar is used to hedge a short underlying position.

You have a short futures position with the futures contract currently trading at a price close to 160. You would like to hedge your position with a collar.

a. Which of the following positions will serve as a hedge?

_____ long a 170 call / short a 150 put

_____ long a 150 call / short a 170 put

_____ short a 170 call / long a 150 put

_____ short a 150 call / long a 170 put

_____ long a 165 call / short a 145 put

_____ long a 145 call / short a 165 put

_____ short a 165 call / long a 145 put

_____ short a 145 call / long a 165 put

_____ long a 175 call / short a 155 put

_____ long a 155 call / short a 175 put

_____ short a 175 call / long a 155 put

_____ short a 155 call / long a 175 put

b. From the selected strategies in part a, which strategies would you prefer if implied volatility is low (all options seem cheap)?

c. From the selected strategies in part b, which do you think will be easiest to execute in the marketplace?

4. A producer of a commodity is a *natural long*: any increase in the commodity price will benefit the producer, while any decline in the price will hurt. A producer can set a price *floor* by purchasing a put option. When it comes time to sell the commodity, the producer will never receive less than the put's exercise price.

An end user of a commodity is a *natural short*: any decline in the commodity price will benefit the end user, while any increase in the price will hurt. An end user can set a price *ceiling* by purchasing a call option. When it comes time to purchase the commodity, the end user will never pay more than the call's exercise price.

You are an end user of a commodity who requires delivery of the commodity in July. The current price for a July futures contract is 496.50. The following options are also available:

option	July 525 call	July 550 call	July 450 put	July 475 put
price	10.25	5.00	4.75	11.50

a. Using only single contracts, from the above list what are the possible hedging choices?

b. Ignoring transaction costs and any interest considerations, for each of the possible strategies, what will be your total commodity cost at July expiration?

STRATEGY	TOTAL COST

c. On the following grids, plot the total cost involving call strategies (one grid) and the total cost involving put strategies (another grid).

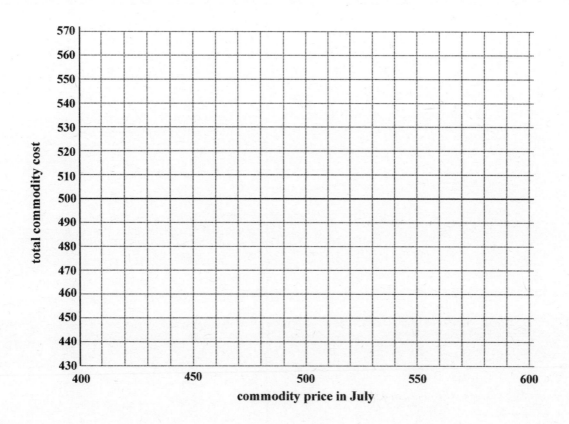

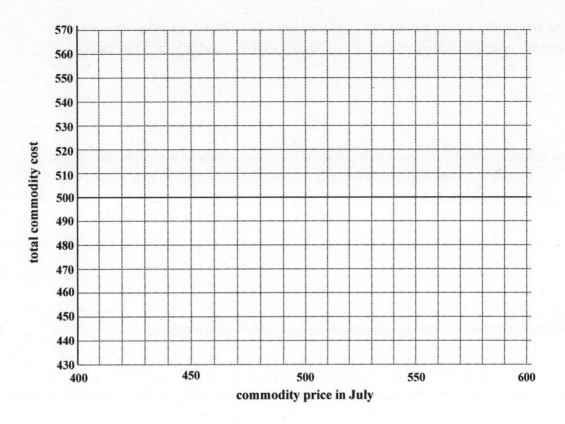

In addition to protective options and covered options, a hedge can combine the two strategies, simultaneously buying a protective option and selling a covered option. This will create a collar.

d. Suppose you simultaneously buy a July 525 call and sell a July 475 put. Ignoring transaction costs and any interest considerations, what will be your total commodity cost at July expiration?

e. Instead of buying a July 525 call and selling a July 475 put, you decide to buy a July 550 call and sell a July 450 put. Ignoring transaction costs and any interest considerations, what will be your total commodity cost at July expiration?

f. On the following grid, plot the total commodity cost for both of these strategies.

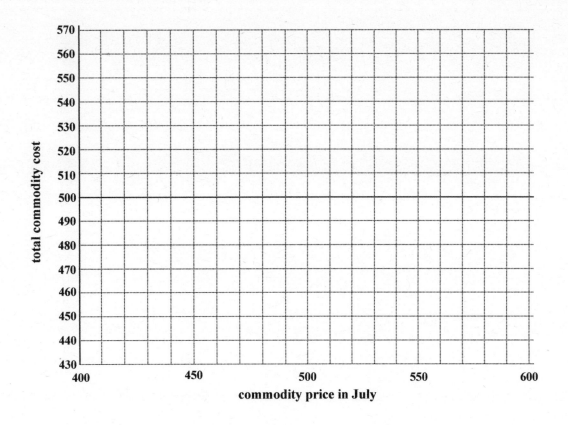

5. You own stock that is currently trading at 63.50. In order to hedge against a decline in the stock price you decide to buy a three-month put with an exercise price of 60. Unfortunately, you find that no such put is listed on any exchange. If your goal is still to buy the 60 put, in theory what can you do?

| CHAPTER 17 |

Models and the Real World

1. The original Black-Scholes model is based on certain assumptions, even if those assumptions may not always be realistic. For each statement below, mark the statement true (T) if it is part of the Black-Scholes framework. Mark the statement false (F) if the statement does not apply.

   a. _____ The prices of the underlying contract at expiration are normally distributed.

   b. _____ The prices of the underlying contract at expiration are lognormally distributed.

   c. _____ The percent changes in the price of the underlying contract are normally distributed.

   d. _____ The percent changes in the price of the underlying contract are lognormally distributed.

   e. _____ The mean of the underlying price distribution at expiration is always equal to the current price of the underlying contract.

   f. _____ The volatility of the underlying contract is constant over the life of the option.

   g. _____ Interest rates are constant over the life of the option.

   h. _____ Over the life of an option the volatility of the underlying contract may change, depending on which direction the market is moving.

   i. _____ There is an optimal time to exercise an option early.

j. _____ The underlying contract can be bought or sold, without restriction, at any time over the life of the option.

k. _____ The price of an underlying contract follows a jump-diffusion process, with occasional gaps in the prices.

l. _____ If held to expiration, the theoretical value of an option is determined by its implied volatility.

2. For each of the statements below, fill in the blank with one of the following phrases:

less often than   **about equal to**   **more often than**

a. For exchange-traded contracts, small price changes (less than one standard deviation) tend to occur in the real world _____ a true normal distribution.

b. For exchange-traded contracts, intermediate price changes (between one and three standard deviations) tend to occur in the real world _____ a true normal distribution.

c. For exchange-traded contracts, large price changes (more than three standard deviations) tend to occur in the real world _____ a true normal distribution.

d. Suppose you know the true volatility of an underlying contract. If you use this volatility in a traditional theoretical pricing model, the value generated for a far out-of-the-money option will tend to be   *(choose one)*   **lower than**   **equal to**   **higher than**   the actual value of the option in the real world.

3. A trader in a futures option market owns an at-the-money straddle. For each of the statements below, fill in the blank with one of the following phrases:

negative   approximately neutral   positive

a. Under the assumptions of a Black-Scholes model, the trader's delta position is

_____.

b. If the futures market tends to become more volatile as prices rise, the trader's delta position is

_____.

c. If the futures market tends to become more volatile as prices fall, the trader's delta position is

_____.

4. For each question below, choose the appropriate answer.

a. A gap in the price of the underlying market will have the greatest effect on the value of an

(choose one)   **in-the-money option   at-the-money option   out-of-the-money option.**

b. A gap in the price of the underlying market will have a greater effect on the value of a

(choose one)   **long-term in-the-money option   short-term in-the-money option.**

c. A gap in the price of the underlying market will have a greater effect on the value of a

(choose one)   **long-term at-the-money option   short-term at-the-money option.**

d. A price gap in the underlying market will work to the benefit of

(choose one)   **a long option position   a short option position.**

e. In most option markets implied volatility derived from a traditional theoretical pricing model tends to be   *(choose one)*   **lower than   equal to   higher than**   the volatility of the underlying contract.

5. Suppose a trader is using a traditional theoretical pricing model to generate option values in a certain market.

    a. In order to generate values that more closely reflect the real world, which of the following is the trader most likely to do? *(Choose all that apply.)*

        _____ Vary the time to expiration used to evaluate different options, even if all options actually expire at the same time.

        _____ Vary the underlying price used to evaluate different options, even if all options have the same underlying contract.

        _____ Vary the volatility used to evaluate different options, even if all options expire at the same time and have the same underlying contract.

    b. In a volatility skew implied volatilities vary across exercise prices, even when all options have the same underlying contract and expiration date.

    Match the primary types of volatility skews below with the characteristics most commonly associated with that skew.

1. balanced skew

A. lower exercise prices have higher implied volatilities and higher exercise prices have lower implied volatilities than at-the-money options.

2. investment skew (stock or stock indexes)

B. lower exercise prices have lower implied volatilities and higher exercise prices have higher implied volatilities than at-the-money options.

3. demand skew (energy products or agricultural commodities)

C. All exercise prices have the same implied volatility.

D. Both lower and higher exercise prices have higher implied volatilities than at-the-money options.

| **CHAPTER 18** |

Skewness and Kurtosis

In order to generate theoretical values that more closely approximate option prices in the marketplace, a trader may vary volatilities across exercise prices, thereby creating a *volatility skew*. The skew is often expressed as a mathematical function with at least two inputs: the skewness (the slope of the volatility skew) and the kurtosis (the curvature of the volatility skew).

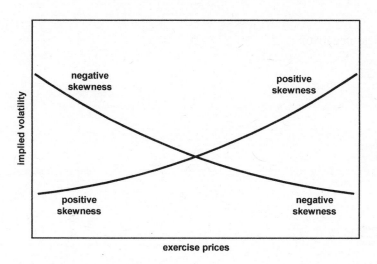

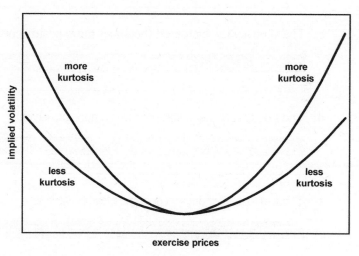

In the following questions you are using an option pricing model that requires a volatility, skew, and kurtosis input. All options are sensitive to changes in the volatility input. The ±25 delta options are most sensitive to changes in the skewness input, and the ±5 delta options are most sensitive to changes in the kurtosis input. The at-the-money (±50 delta) options are not affected by changes in skewness or kurtosis.

1. For each group of options below, will the given change cause the option to rise in value (+), fall in value (–), or remain unchanged (0)? If more than one option will change in the same direction, which option will change most (++ or – –)? Assume that all options expire at the same time.

a. The volatility is increased:

CALL WITH DELTA OF +50	PUT WITH DELTA OF –25	CALL WITH DELTA OF +5

b. The skewness is reduced (becomes less positive or more negative):

PUT WITH DELTA OF –50	PUT WITH DELTA OF –25	CALL WITH DELTA OF +25

c. The skewness is increased (becomes more positive or less negative):

PUT WITH DELTA OF –25	PUT WITH DELTA OF –5	CALL WITH DELTA OF +5

d. The kurtosis is increased (becomes more positive):

PUT WITH DELTA OF –5	CALL WITH DELTA OF +25	PUT WITH DELTA OF –50

e. The kurtosis is reduced (becomes less positive):

PUT WITH DELTA OF –5	PUT WITH DELTA OF –25	CALL WITH A DELTA OF +50

f. Time passes:

PUT WITH DELTA OF –50	CALL WITH DELTA OF +25	PUT WITH DELTA OF –5

2. Suppose your model is generating values that differ from the observed prices in the marketplace for options with delta values given below. The wording describes your model values compared to market prices.

What changes (increase, reduce, leave unchanged) would you need to make to the volatility, skewness, and kurtosis inputs in order to generate model prices that are more consistent with the actual market prices?

a.

−5	−25	−50 / 50	+25	+5
higher	higher	equal to	lower	lower

b.

−5	−25	−50 / 50	+25	+5
higher	higher	higher	higher	higher

c.

−5	−25	−50 / 50	+25	+5
lower	lower	equal to	lower	lower

d.

−5	−25	−50 / 50	+25	+5
equal to	equal to	lower	equal to	equal to

e.

−5	−25	−50 / 50	+25	+5
equal to	equal to	higher	much higher	much higher

3. You have an option position that is delta neutral and is also short skew (you want the skewness to become less positive or more negative).

   a. Which of the following positions fits the above description? (There may be more than one choice.)

       _____ long in-the-money puts / short in-the-money calls / short underlying contracts

       _____ long out-of-the-money puts / short out-of-the-money calls / long underlying contracts

       _____ short in-the-money puts / long in-the-money calls / long underlying contracts

       _____ short in-the-money puts / long in-the-money calls / short underlying contracts

       _____ long out-of-the-money puts / short out-of-the-money calls / short underlying contracts

       _____ long in-the-money puts / short in-the-money calls / long underlying contracts

Suppose your position (delta neutral / short skew) is a stock option position that consists primarily of out-of-the-money calls and out-of-the-money puts together with a stock position.

   b. If the price of the underlying stock begins to rise, what will happen to your *gamma* position? (get longer, get shorter, remain unchanged)

   c. If the price of the underlying stock begins to fall, what will happen to your *vega* position? (get longer, get shorter, remain unchanged)

d. If two weeks pass with no change in the stock price, what will happen to your *delta* position? (get longer, get shorter, remain unchanged)

e. If implied volatility rises, what will happen to your *delta* position? (get longer, get shorter, remain unchanged)

f. What combination of stock direction (up or down), changes in implied volatility (rising or falling), changes in interest rates (rising or falling), and changes in dividends (increase or decrease) will most help this position if:

    i. the market moves very quickly

    ii. the market moves very slowly

CHAPTER 19
Stock Indexes

The three most common methods of constructing a stock index are price-weighting, capitalization-weighting, and equal-weighting.

In a price-weighted index the initial value of the index is equal to the sum of the prices of the individual stocks that make up the index.

$$\text{price-weighted index value} = \Sigma S_i$$

In a capitalization-weighted index the initial value of the index is equal to the sum of the capitalizations of the individual companies that make up the index. The capitalization of a company is equal to the total value of all outstanding stock in that company.

$$\text{capitalization-weighted index value} = \Sigma(S_i \times \text{number of shares outstanding})$$

In an equal-weighted index, each stock initially accounts for exactly an equal proportion of the index. So the index value is initially equal to the number of stocks which make up the index.

$$\text{equal-weighted index value} = \Sigma(S_i / S_i)$$

As stock prices change, the contribution of each stock will change by the percent change in each stock's price.

$$\text{equal-weighted index value} = \Sigma(S_{\text{current price}} / S_{\text{previous price}})$$

Equal-weighted indexes are periodically rebalanced so that each stock again accounts for exactly an equal proportion of the index.

The weighting of a stock in an index is the amount of the index, in percent terms, accounted for by that stock. The index divisor is a number used to set the raw value of an index equal to a target value or reference value:

$$\text{raw index value} / \text{divisor} = \text{target value}$$

1. When the XYZ index is initially introduced, it is made up of the following three stocks:

STOCK	STOCK PRICE	OUTSTANDING SHARES
X	25.30	9000
Y	81.70	5000
Z	46.55	3000

a. What is the value of the index and the weighting of each stock in the index if the index is:

i. price-weighted?

X	
Y	
Z	

ii. capitalization-weighted?

X	
Y	
Z	

iii. equal-weighted?

X	
Y	
Z	

b. Suppose the index is initially set at a value of 250. What is the index divisor if the index is:

   i. price-weighted?

   ii. capitalization-weighted?

   iii. equal-weighted?

c. With the index value still at 250, stock Y splits 2 for 1: every old share of stock Y at a price of 81.70 is replaced with two new shares at a price of 40.85 each. If the index value remains unchanged at 250, what must be the new index divisor if the index is:

   i. price-weighted?

   ii. capitalization-weighted?

   iii. equal-weighted?

d. Following the 2 for 1 split in stock Y, and with the index price still at 250, stock Z is replaced with stock W, with a price of 34.85 and 6000 outstanding shares. What must be the new index divisor if the index is:

   i. price-weighted?

  ii. capitalization-weighted?

 iii. equal-weighted?

e. Assume that the equal-weighted index is still made up of the original three stocks, X, Y, and Z. At some later date, the prices of the stocks are:

STOCK	STOCK PRICE
X	26.54
Y	80.25
Z	48.93

i. What is the current value of the equal-weighted index?

ii. If the index is now rebalanced, such that each stock has an equal weighting in the index, what is the new index divisor?

2. When the price of an index component stock changes, then:

percent change in the index = percent change in the stock price × stock weighting in the index

An index is currently trading at 12,599.83. Among the component stocks in the index are stock A and stock B, with the following prices and weightings in the index:

STOCK	PRICE	WEIGHTING
A	186.50	8.64%
B	98.75	5.12%

a. If the price of stock A rises 4.00 to 190.50, and all other stocks in the index remain unchanged, what will be the new index price?

b. After rising to 190.50 stock A subsequently falls 12.00 to 178.50. At the same time stock B rises 2.75 to 101.50. What will be the new index price if all other stocks in the index remain unchanged?

c. When stock A rises from 186.50 to 190.50, what must be its new weighting in the index if all other stocks in the index remain unchanged?

3. The LMN index is made up of the following three stocks:

STOCK	STOCK PRICE	WEIGHTING
L	30.25	25.29%
M	70.81	42.63%
N	55.46	32.08%

a. A fund manager has $1,000,000 to invest and would like his holdings to exactly replicate the index. How many shares of each stock must he buy?

L	
M	
N	

b. Instead of replicating the index, a fund manager wants to offset a short position equal to $1,000,000 in three-month index futures contracts. How many shares of each stock must he hold if interest rates are 6.00%?

L	
M	
N	

c. Two months later interest rates have fallen to 5.40%. If the fund manager is still holding his short index futures position, how many shares of each stock must he now hold in order to offset his short futures position?

L	
M	
N	

4. An index futures contract with 72 days remaining to expiration is trading at 2,520.37.

a. If interest rates are 5.33% and the expected dividend over the next 72 days is 9.94 index points, what should be the index cash price?

b. If the index cash price is currently 2,509.80 and the expected dividend over the next 72 days is 9.94 index points, what is the implied interest rate?

c. If the index cash price is currently 2,507.94 and interest rates are 3.83%, what is the implied dividend payout in index points over the next 72 days?

CHAPTER 20

Risk Analysis

1. Before the age of computer technology and the widespread use of theoretical pricing models, traders were sometimes able to analyze the risk of a position by rewriting a position in a more easily identifiable form using synthetic equivalents.

   You have the following position:

   +12 October 45 calls

   −87 October 45 puts

   −46 October 50 calls

   +46 October 50 puts

   +59 October 55 calls

   +16 October 55 puts

   −25 underlying contracts

   a. Using synthetic equivalents, what is your delta, gamma, theta, and vega position (positive, negative, or neutral) if the underlying contract is trading at a price close to 45?

b. What is your delta, gamma, theta, and vega position (positive, negative, or neutral) if the underlying contract is trading at a price close to 55?

2. In the stock option market, when a stock splits "y" shares for "x" shares (e.g., in a 2 for 1 stock split, the holder of each old share receives 2 of the new shares), the following adjustments apply:

new stock price: old stock price × "x" / "y"

underlying contract: unchanged (typically 100 shares)

for each option:

new exercise price: old exercise price × "x" / "y"

new option position: old option position × "y" / "x"

new option price: old option price / ("y" / "x")

new option delta: same as old option delta

new option gamma: old option gamma × ("y" / "x")

new option theta: old option theta / ("y" / "x")

new option vega: old option vega / ("y" / "x")

new option rho: old option rho / ("y" / "x")

You have the following option position on a stock that is currently trading at a price of 122.82, where the underlying contract consists of 100 shares of stock:

+68 November 120 puts

+37 November 135 calls

+1200 shares of stock

The sensitivities of the options are:

	DELTA	GAMMA	THETA	VEGA	RHO
November 120 put	−36.3	2.41	−.0189	.264	−.162
November 135 call	28.1	2.17	−.0252	.240	+.105

a. What is your total delta, gamma, theta, vega, and rho position?

  i. delta:

  ii. gamma:

iii. theta:

iv. vega:

v. rho:

b. The company announces a 3 for 1 stock split: every old share of stock will be replaced with three new shares. After the stock split takes effect, what is the new stock price?

c. After the stock split, what will be your new option and stock position?

d. After the stock split, approximately, what are the new delta, gamma, theta, vega, and rho values for the new options?

	DELTA	GAMMA	THETA	VEGA	RHO
new put					
new call					

e. After the stock split, what is your total delta, gamma, theta, vega, and rho position?

  i. **total** delta:

  ii. **total** gamma:

    iii. total theta:

    iv. total vega:

    v. total rho:

f. Can you identify the relationships between the total delta, gamma, theta, vega, and rho position before and after the stock split?

    i. new delta position:

ii. new gamma position:

iii. new theta position:

iv. new vega position:

v. new rho position:

g. Suppose that prior to the stock split the prices of the November 120 put and the November 135 call were 4.14 and 2.55, respectively. At their new exercise prices, what will be their approximate prices after the split?

3. In an option market with multiple expirations, when implied volatility changes it rarely changes by an equal amount across all expirations. More often, the implied volatility of short-term expirations will change more quickly than the implied volatility of long-term expirations. This is a characteristic of the *term structure of volatility*, where the implied volatility of long-term expirations tends to remain close to the mean, or average, volatility of that particular market.

Suppose there are four expiration months trading at the following implied volatilities:

TIME TO EXPIRATION	1 MONTH	3 MONTHS	6 MONTHS	12 MONTHS
implied volatility	33%	30%	28%	27%

a. Which of the following is the best estimate of the mean volatility in this market?

     26%   29%   33%   37%

b. If 1-month implied volatility falls to 30%, which of the following is a logical implied volatility scenario? (*Choose one of i–iv.*)

	1-MONTH	3-MONTH	6-MONTH	12-MONTH
i.	30%	30%	30%	30%
ii.	30%	27%	25%	24%
iii.	30%	28%	27%	26%
iv.	30%	27%	27%	27%

c. If 1-month implied volatility rises to 37%, which of the following is a logical implied volatility scenario? (*Choose one of i–v.*)

	1-MONTH	3-MONTH	6-MONTH	12-MONTH
i.	37%	33%	30%	28%
ii.	37%	34%	32%	31%
iii.	37%	34%	33%	32%
iv.	37%	40%	42%	43%

3. Because implied volatilities do not change at the same rate across all expirations, if we want an accurate picture of the vega risk for a portfolio consisting of multiple expirations it will be necessary to adjust the vega values to reflect the different rates at which implied volatility changes. This is often done by making no adjustment to the front month vega, but by multiplying the vega of each subsequent expiration by an adjustment factor based on how fast the implied volatility changes compared to the front month.

a. Consider a position consisting of four expiration months with each month's total vega values.

EXPIRATION	MARCH	APRIL	JUNE	SEPTEMBER
vega	−23.10	+13.10	−14.20	+28.40

i. If we make no adjustments, what is the total vega position?

ii. Would this position prefer implied volatility to rise or fall?

b. Suppose we have determined that implied volatility for April tends to change at 80% of the rate of change in March implied volatility, implied volatility for June tends to change at 70% of the rate of change in March, and implied volatility for September tends to change at 65% of the rate of change in March.

i. In terms of changes in March implied volatility, what is the total adjusted vega for the position?

EXPIRATION MONTH	VEGA	ADJUSTMENT	TOTAL ADJUSTED VEGA
March			
April			
June			
September			
Totals			

ii. Based on your total adjusted vega, would the position prefer implied volatility to rise or fall?

iii. If implied volatility in March rises three percentage points, how will the position P&L be affected?

4. The term structure of volatility in an option market can be an important consideration, not only in evaluating risk, but also in trying to identify potential trading strategies.

Consider these implied volatilities across expirations in an option market:

TIME TO EXPIRATION (WEEKS)	IMPLIED VOLATILITY (%) (AT-THE-MONEY OPTIONS)
2	19.80
4	20.51
9	21.20
13	21.70
26	22.80
39	23.06
52	23.46
78	23.55
104	23.70

a. On the grid below, as best you can, plot the implied volatilities for the various expirations.

Can you identify any expirations where the implied volatilities seem to be mispriced, at least in relation to other expirations? To help you identify any mispricings, you may want to draw a curve that seems to best fit the implied volatility points.

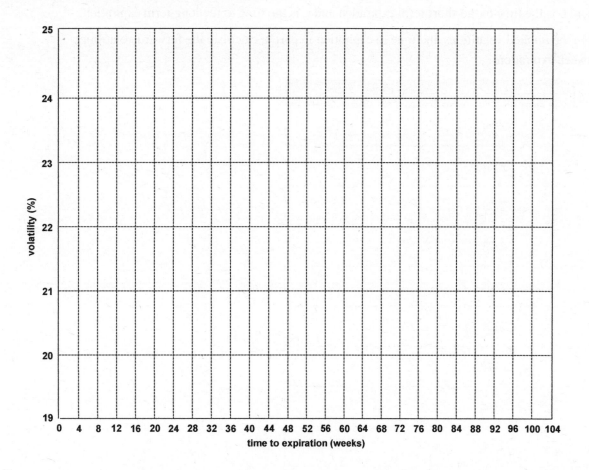

b. If we know a short-term implied volatility (σ_1) and a long-term implied volatility (σ_2), we can calculate the *forward volatility* (σ_f), the volatility that is expected to occur between the short-term and long-term expirations:

$$\sigma_f = \sqrt{\{[(\sigma_2^2 \times t_2) - (\sigma_1^2 \times t_1)]/(t_2 - t_1)\}}$$

where t_1 is the time to the short-term expiration and t_2 is the time to the long-term expiration.

From the implied volatilities and time to expiration in part a, calculate the forward volatilities between expirations.

TIME TO EXPIRATION (WEEKS)	IMPLIED VOLATILITY (%) (AT-THE-MONEY OPTIONS)	FORWARD VOLATILITY
2	19.80	
4	20.51	
9	21.20	
13	21.70	
26	22.80	
39	23.06	
52	23.46	
78	23.55	
104	23.70	

Now go back and overlay the forward volatilities on your plot of the implied volatilities. Is it easier to see which expirations are mispriced? You can also connect the forward volatility plot points to form a *forward volatility curve*.

5. A detailed risk analysis of any complex option position will almost certainly require a reliable theoretical pricing model, as well as software that can analyze the position under a wide variety of market conditions, including changes in underlying price, volatility, and time to expiration. However, if we know the sensitivities of a position (delta, gamma, etc.), as well as the number of contracts that make up the position, it is often possible to do a preliminary risk analysis by asking several basic questions about the position.

Consider the following stock and stock option position consisting of two expiration months:

OPTIONS	TOTAL CALLS	TOTAL PUTS	TOTAL DELTA	TOTAL GAMMA	TOTAL THETA	TOTAL VEGA	TOTAL RHO
Month 1	+53	+16	+4610	+25	−2.57	+4.5	+14.4
Month 2	−80	+64	−3484	−41	+3.30	−20.2	−25.7
totals	−27	+80	+326	−16	+.73	−15.7	−11.3

where the delta and gamma are given in the whole number format, the theta is the decay per one day's passage of time, the vega is the sensitivity to a one percentage point change in volatility, and the rho is the sensitivity to a one percentage point change in interest rates.

Note that no prices or theoretical values are given for any of the contracts that make up the position. A position can be initiated at favorable or unfavorable prices (usually compared to model generated values). But once a trader has taken on a position the risk characteristics of the position are independent of the prices.

From the above values, try to answer the following questions:

a. Looking at the delta, gamma, vega, and rho, what is the best and worst scenario for the position?

   i. Best scenario:

   ii. Worst scenario:

b. Considering the delta and gamma, estimate the stock price (compared to the current stock price) at which the position will show its maximum theoretical profit. (Hint: a negative gamma position will show its maximum value when it is delta neutral.)

c. Suppose that the entire position was evaluated using a volatility of 22%, and at this volatility the position has a positive theoretical edge (compared to the current market prices) of 78 points. From the vega, what is the implied volatility of the entire position? In other words, at what volatility will the position have a theoretical edge of zero?

d. Using the current theoretical edge of 78 points, if the stock moves up or down 10 points, what will be the new theoretical edge for the position?

e. Suppose that the market makes such a large move that all options are either very deeply in-the-money or very far out-of-the money. In terms of underlying contracts, what will be the characteristics of the position if the move is . . .

    i. downward?

ii. upward?

f. How does your answer to question 5e.i above compare to your answer to question 5a?

g. The total delta position is currently +326. Suppose there is a dramatic increase in implied volatility. How will this affect the total delta position?

h. In question 5c we made the assumption that the entire position was evaluated using a single volatility of 22%. But we know that this is not always true. Due to the term structure of volatility different months are often evaluated using different volatilities, and these volatilities will often change at different rates.

Suppose that volatility in Month 2 tends to change at 75% of the rate of change in Month 1 volatility. That is, if volatility changes by one percentage point in Month 1, it will change by .75 percentage point in Month 2.

i. In terms of Month 1 volatility, what is the total adjusted vega for the position?

ii. Using the adjusted vega, if, as in question c, the Month 1 implied volatility is 22%, what is the implied volatility of the entire position in terms of the Month 1 volatility?

i. Suppose a dividend of 3.00 is expected to be paid after Month 1 expiration but prior to Month 2 expiration. If the dividend is unexpectedly increased to 5.00, how will this affect the potential profit or loss from the entire position?

Useful Formulas and Relationships

In the following,

S = stock price or spot price

F = forward price or price of a futures contract

X = exercise price

r = annual interest rate

t = time to expiration or time to maturity, in years

σ = annual volatility

D = expected dividends to maturity for a stock (but excluding interest on the dividends)

The Forward Price (F)

	SIMPLE INTEREST	CONTINUOUS INTEREST
for a stock	$F = S \times (1 + r \times t) - D$	$F = S \times e^{r \times t} - D$
for a foreign currency	$F = S \times (1 + r_d \times t) / (1 + r_f \times t)$	$F = S\, e^{(r_d - r_f) \times t}$

where
r_d = domestic interest rate
r_f = foreign interest rate

Volatility (σ)

	SIMPLE CALCULATION	CONTINUOUS COMPOUNDING
a price range of n standard deviations at the end of time, t	$F \times (1 \pm n \times \sigma \times \sqrt{t})$	$F \times e^{\pm(n \times \sigma \times \sqrt{t})}$

Probabilities (Approximate)

68¼% of all occurrences fall within one standard deviation of the mean.

95½% of all occurrences fall within two standard deviations of the mean.

99¾% of all occurrences fall within three standard deviations of the mean.

The "Greeks"

Delta (Δ). The sensitivity of an option's theoretical value to a change in the underlying price.

Gamma (Γ). The sensitivity of an option's delta to a change in the underlying price; usually expressed as the change in delta per one point change in the underlying price.

Theta (Θ). The sensitivity of an option's theoretical value to the passage of time; usually expressed as the change in value per one day's passage of time.

Vega. The sensitivity of an option's theoretical value to a change in volatility; usually expressed as the change in value per one percentage point (1.00%) change in volatility. Often interpreted as the sensitivity of an option's price to a change in implied volatility.

Rho (P). The sensitivity of an option's theoretical value to a change in interest rates; usually expressed as the change in value per one percentage point (1.00%) change in interest rates.

Spreading Strategies

VOLATILITY SPREADS (all spreads assumed to be delta neutral)	DELTA	GAMMA	THETA	VEGA	UPSIDE RISK/REWARD	DOWNSIDE RISK/REWARD
long straddle	0	+	−	+	unlimited reward	unlimited reward
short straddle	0	−	+	−	unlimited risk	unlimited risk
long strangle	0	+	−	+	unlimited reward	unlimited reward
short strangle	0	−	+	−	unlimited risk	unlimited risk
long butterfly	0	−	+	−	limited risk	limited risk
short butterfly	0	+	−	+	limited reward	limited reward
long condor	0	−	+	−	limited risk	limited risk
short condor	0	+	−	+	limited reward	limited reward
call ratio spread—buy more than sell	0	+	−	+	unlimited reward	limited reward
call ratio spread—sell more than buy	0	−	+	−	unlimited risk	limited risk
put ratio spread—buy more than sell	0	+	−	+	limited reward	unlimited reward
put ratio spread—sell more than buy	0	−	+	−	limited risk	unlimited risk
long calendar spread	0	−	+	+	limited risk	limited risk
short calendar spread	0	+	−	−	limited reward	limited reward
DIRECTIONAL SPREADS						
bull spread (long call spread or short put spread)						
long exercise price is closer to at-the-money	+	+	−	+	limited reward	limited risk
short exercise price is closer to at-the-money	+	−	+	−	limited reward	limited risk
bear spread (short call spread or long put spread)						
long exercise price is closer to at-the-money	−	+	−	+	limited risk	limited reward
short exercise price is closer to at-the-money	−	−	+	−	limited risk	limited reward

Synthetic Relationships

The six basic synthetic long and short contracts; all options have the same exercise price and expiration date:

long call + short put ≈ long underlying contract

short call + long put ≈ short underlying contract

long put + long underlying contract ≈ long call

short put + short underlying contract ≈ short call

long call + short underlying contract ≈ long put

short call + long underlying contract ≈ short put

box = synthetic long underlying contract at one exercise price + synthetic short underlying contract at a different exercise price where all options expire at the same time

= bull call spread + bear put spread

roll = synthetic long underlying contract at one expiration date + synthetic short underlying contract at a different expiration date where all options have the same exercise price

= call calendar spread – put calendar spread

Arbitrage Relationships for European Options

	SIMPLE INTEREST	CONTINUOUS INTEREST
put-call parity:		
call price − put price =	$(F-X)/(1+r{\times}t)$	$(F-X){\times}e^{-r{\times}t}$
for a stock which pays no dividend	$S-X/(1+r{\times}t)$	$S-X{\times}e^{-r{\times}t}$
an approximation for stock options	$S-X+X{\times}r{\times}t-D$	
box value:	$(X_{higher}-X_{lower})/(1+r{\times}t)$	$(X_{higher}-X_{lower}){\times}e^{-r{\times}t}$
roll value:	$[(F_1-X)/(1+r_1{\times}t_1)]-[(F_2-X)/(1+r_2{\times}t_2)]-D$	$(F_1-X){\times}e^{-r1{\times}t2}-(F_2-X){\times}e^{-r2{\times}t2}-D$
an approximation for stock options:	$X{\times}r{\times}(t_2-t_1)-D$	
delta:		
for options on stock	$|\Delta_c|+|\Delta_p|=100$	$|\Delta_c|+|\Delta_p|=100$
for options on futures; subject to stock-type settlement	$|\Delta_c|+|\Delta_p|=100/(1+r{\times}t)$	$|\Delta_c|+|\Delta_p|=100{\times}e^{-r{\times}t}$
gamma:	$\Gamma_c=\Gamma_p$	$\Gamma_c=\Gamma_p$
vega:	$vega_c=vega_p$	$vega_c=vega_p$

Criteria for Early Exercise

Criteria must apply over the entire life of the option as well as over the next day.

For a stock option call:	$D>X{\times}r{\times}t+$ call volatility value $\approx X{\times}r{\times}t+$ price of the companion out-of-the-money put
For a stock option put:	$X{\times}r{\times}t>D+$ put volatility value $\approx D+$ price of the companion out-of-the-money call
For a futures option where the option is subject to stock-type settlement:	Intrinsic value $\times r{\times}t>$ volatility value $\approx$ price of the companion out-of-the-money option
In all cases:	One day's worth of volatility value $\approx$ the theta of the companion out-of-the-money option

Black-Scholes Model

For the complete Black-Scholes model refer to Chapter 14.

Binomial Option Pricing

	SIMPLE CALCULATION	CONTINUOUS COMPOUNDING
an upward move, S_u, where $u =$	$1 + \sigma \times \sqrt{t}$	$e^{\sigma \times \sqrt{t}}$
a downward move, S_d, where $d =$	$1 / (1 + \sigma \times \sqrt{t})$	$e^{-\sigma \times \sqrt{t}}$
the probability, p, of an upward move to S_u		
for stock	$[(1 + r \times t) - d] / (u - d)$	$(e^{r \times t} - d) / (u - d)$
for a futures contract	$(1 - d) / (u - d)$	$(1 - d) / (u - d)$
the probability of a downward move, in all cases $= 1 - p$		
terminal values for a call, C:	maximum of $[S - X, 0]$	
terminal values for a put, P:	maximum of $[X - S, 0]$	
for a binomial tree of n periods, the value of an option, O, at any point along the binomial tree	$(p \times O_u + (1 - p)O_d)/(1 + r \times t/n)$	$(p \times O_u + (1 - p)O_d) \times e^{-r \times t/n}$
the delta, Δ, of an option, O (either a call or put)	$(O_u - O_d) / (S_u - S_d)$	
the gamma, Γ, of an option, O (either a call or put)	$(\Delta_u - \Delta_d) / (S_u - S_d)$	
the theta, Θ, of an option, O (either a call or put)	$(O_n - O_{n+2}) / (2 \times t/n)$	

Answer Key

CHAPTER 1

Contract Settlement and Cash Flow

1. a.

TRADE SEQUENCE	STOCK PRICE	TRADE	OPEN SHARE POSITION	CASH FLOW CREDIT (+) OR DEBIT (−)	CUMULATIVE CASH CREDIT (+) OR DEBIT (−)	CUMULATIVE PROFIT (+) OR LOSS (−)		TOTAL CUMULATIVE PROFIT (+) OR LOSS (−)
						REALIZED	UNREALIZED	
1 (initial trade)	$46.78	buy 3000 shares	long 3000	−$140,340.00 300×-46.78	−$140,340.00	0	0	0
2	$45.91	buy 1000 shares	long 4000	−$45,910.00 1000×-45.91	−$186,250.00	0	−$2,610.00 $3,000 \times (45.91 - 46.78)$	−$2,610.00
3	$47.63	sell 1200 shares	long 2800	+$57,156.00 1200×47.63	−$129,094.00	+$1,020.00 $1,200 \times (47.63 - 46.78)$	+$3,250.00 $1,800 \times (47.63 - 46.78)$ $+ 1,000 \times (47.63 - 45.91)$	+$4,270.00
4	$46.15	buy 500 shares	long 3300	−$23,075.00	−$152,169.00	+$1,020.00	−$894.00 $1,800 \times (46.15 - 46.78)$ $+ 1,000 \times (46.15 - 45.91)$	+$126.00
5	$49.20	sell 1100 shares	long 2200	+$54,120.00	−$98,049.00	+3,682.00 $1,020.00$ $+ 1,100 \times (49.20 - 46.78)$	+$6,509.00 $700 \times (49.20 - 46.78)$ $+ 1,000 \times (49.20 - 45.91)$ $+ 500 \times (49.20 - 46.15)$	+$10,191.00
6	$48.55	sell 700 shares	long 1500	+$33,985.00	−$64,064.00	+$4,921.00 $3,682.00$ $+ 700 \times (48.55 - 46.78)$	+$3,840.00 $1,000 \times (48.55 - 45.91)$ $+ 500 \times (48.55 - 46.15)$	+8,761.00
7	$48.08	sell 1500 shares	0	+$72,120.00	+$8,056.00	+$8,056.00 $4,921.00$ $+ 1,000 \times 500 \times (48.08 - 46.15)(48.08 - 45.91)$	0	+8,056.00

b.

PERIOD	CASH POSITION AT BEGINNING OF PERIOD	INTEREST CREDIT (+) OR DEBIT (−) OVER THE PERIOD
1	−$140,340.00	−$140,340.00 × .06/12 = −$701.70
2	−$186,250.00	−$186,250.00 × .06/12 = −$931.25
3	−$129,094.00	−$129,094.00 × .06/12 = −$645.47
4	−$152,169.00	−$152,169.00 × .06/12 = −$760.85
5	−$98,049.00	−$98,049.00 × .06/12 = −$490.25
6	−$64,064.00	−$64,064.00 × .06/12 = −$320.32

c. Total interest: **−$3,849.84**

d. +$8,056.00 − $3,849.84 = **+$4,206.16**

Interest costs can significantly reduce the profits of a stock trade, especially in a high interest rate environment.

2. a. What is the notional value of the contract?

625.80 × $200 = **$125,160.00**

b.

TRADE SEQUENCE	FUTURES PRICE	TRADE	OPEN FUTURES POSITION	MARGIN REQUIREMENT	CASH FLOW (VARIATION) CREDIT (+) OR DEBIT (−)	CUMULATIVE PROFIT (+) OR LOSS (−)		TOTAL CUMULATIVE PROFIT (+) OR LOSS (−)
						REALIZED	UNREALIZED	
1	625.80	sell 25	−25	$125,000 25 × $5,000	0	0	0	0
2	621.60	buy 5	−20	$100,000 20 × $5,000	+$21,000.00 −25 × 200 × (621.60 − 625.80)	+$21,000.00	0	+$2,000.00
3	633.00	sell 10	−30	$150,000 30 × $5,000	−$45,600.00 −20 × 200 × (633.00 − 621.60)	−$24,600.00	0	−$24,600.00

(continued on next page)

TRADE SEQUENCE	FUTURES PRICE	TRADE	OPEN FUTURES POSITION	MARGIN REQUIREMENT	CASH FLOW (VARIATION) CREDIT (+) OR DEBIT (−)	CUMULATIVE PROFIT (+) OR LOSS (−)		TOTAL CUMULATIVE PROFIT (+) OR LOSS (−)
						REALIZED	UNREALIZED	
4	617.50	no trade	−30	$150,000	+$93,000.00 −30 × 200 × (617.50 − 633.00)	+$68,400.00	0	+$68,400.00
5	608.90	buy 20	−10	$50,000 10 × $5,000	+$51,600.00 −30 × 200 × (608.90 − 617.50)	+$120,000.00	0	+$120,000.00
6	612.00	sell 5	−15	$75,000 15 × 5,000	−$6,200.00 −10 × 200 × (612.00 − 608.90)	+$113,800.00	0	+$113,800.00
7	619.50	buy 15	0	0	−$22,500.00 −15 × 200 × (619.50 − 612.00)	+$91,300.00	0	+$91,300.00

In futures-type settlement all profits or losses are immediately realized. There are no unrealized profits or losses.

c.

PERIOD	VARIATION CASH AT BEGINNING OF PERIOD	INTEREST CREDIT(+) OR DEBIT(−) ON VARIATION OVER THE NEXT PERIOD
1	0	0
2	+$21,000.00	+$21,000.00 × .078/52 = **+$31.50**
3	−$24,600.00	−$24,600.00 × .078/52 = **−$36.90**
4	+$68,400.00	+$68,400.00 × .078/52 = **+$102.60**
5	+$120,000.00	+$120,000.00 × .078/52 = **+$180.00**
6	+$113,800.00	$113,800.00 × .078/52 = **+$170.70**

d. total variation interest: **+$447.90**

e. Including the interest credit or debit, what is the total profit or loss resulting from the entire series of trades?

+$91,300.00 + $447.90 = **+$91,747.90**

Interest considerations in futures-type settlement are usually less important than in stock-type settlement.

CHAPTER 2

Forward Pricing

1. $F = S \times (1 + rt) - D$

	STOCK PRICE	TIME TO MATURITY	EXPECTED DIVIDENDS	INTEREST RATE	FORWARD PRICE
a.	46.85	2 months	0	4.80%	$46.80 \times (1 + .048/6) = \mathbf{47.22}$
b.	94.66	10 weeks	.50	2.75%	$94.66 \times (1 + .0275 \times 10/52) - .50 = \mathbf{94.66}$
c.	53.28	216 days	.30	6.10%	$53.28 \times (1 + .061 \times 216/365) - .30 = \mathbf{54.90}$
d.	130.00	4 weeks	.75	3.22%	$130.00 \times (1 + .0322 \times 4/52) - .75 = \mathbf{129.57}$
e.	19.70	5 months	.16	8.31%	$19.70 \times (1 + .0831 \times 5/12) - .16 = \mathbf{20.22}$

2. $123.15 \times 1.053 - 2.60 \times (1 + .053 \times 10/12) - 2.60 \times (1+.053 \times 4/12) = \mathbf{124.32}$

3. $S = (F + D) / (1 + rt)$

	FUTURES PRICE	TIME TO MATURITY	EXPECTED DIVIDENDS	INTEREST RATE	STOCK PRICE
a.	39.95	3 months	.10	3.75%	$(39.95 + .10) / (1 + .0375/4) = \mathbf{39.68}$
b.	114.10	19 weeks	.62	7.11%	$(114.10 + .62) / (1+.0711 \times 19/52) = \mathbf{111.82}$
c.	80.76	35 days	.25	5.00%	$(80.76 + .25) / (1+.05 \times 35/365) = \mathbf{80.62}$

4. **a.** $D = S \times (1 + rt) - F = 76.60 \times (1 + .0425 \times 84/365) - 76.95 = \mathbf{.40}$

   b. $r = [(F + D)/S - 1] / t) = [(77.30 + .51)/76.70 - 1]/(84/365) = \mathbf{6.29\%}$

5. a. forward price = cash price × (1 + *rt*) + storage = 463.25 × (1 + .064 × 5/12) + 5 × 2.75 = **489.35**

    b. Buy the commodity now and store it for five months. This will only cost you 489.35. Given the above prices, there may also be an arbitrage opportunity, but that is not your focus. As an end user you want delivery at the lowest possible price.

    c. Buy the futures contract and take delivery of the commodity in five months. This is 9.35 cheaper than buying the commodity yourself and storing it for five months.

    d. Cash price should be: (futures price – storage) / (1 + rt) = (468.50 – 5.50) / (1+.064 × 2/12) = 458.11

        convenience yield = 463.25 – 458.11 = **5.14**

6. $F = S \times (1 + r_d t) / (1 + r_f t)$

    1.24 × (1+.0232/4) / (1+.0378/4) = **1.2355**

Contract Specifications and Terminology

1.

	ACTION	STOCK PRICE	STOCK POSITION	CASH FLOW
a.	you exercise 2 February 70 calls	73.50	+200 shares	−14,000
b.	you exercise 8 April 40 puts	35.25	−800 shares	+32,000
c.	you are assigned on 16 June 55 calls	58.10	−1,600 shares	+88,000
d.	you are assigned on 5 August 120 puts	116.85	+500 shares	−60,000
e.	you exercise 37 October 25 puts	25.00	−3700 shares	+92,500
f.	you are assigned on 21 December 160 calls	183.00	−2100 shares	+336,000

Although the stock price will eventually determine whether an option trade is profitable or not, the stock price is irrelevant to the cash flow resulting from exercise or assignment. The cash flow is determined solely by the option's exercise price.

2.

ACTION	STOCK POSITION	CASH FLOW
you exercise 25 August 75 calls	+2500 shares	−187,500
you exercise 42 August 95 puts	−4200 shares	+399,000
you are assigned on 16 August 80 calls	−1600 shares	+128,000
you are assigned on 51 August 100 puts	+5100 shares	−510,000
totals	+1800 shares	−170,500

3.

	ACTION	FUTURES PRICE	FUTURES POINT VALUE	FUTURES POSITION	CASH FLOW
a.	you exercise 10 January 1300 calls	1,325.00	100	+10 futures	+25,000
b.	you are assigned 3 March 95 calls	98.50	1000	−3 futures	−10,500
c.	you exercise on 21 May 1850 puts	1,832.50	250	−21 futures	+91,875
d.	you are assigned on 65 July 900 puts	866.50	10	+65 futures	−21,775
e.	you exercise 48 September 650 calls	650.00	50	+48 futures	0
f.	you are assigned on 30 December 150 puts	137.50	500	+30 futures	−187,500

When you exercise or are assigned on a futures option, you are buying or selling the futures contract at the exercise price. There is an immediate variation credit or debit equal to the difference between the exercise price and the current futures price.

4. Futures contracts are listed for March, June, September, and December.

	ACTION	FUTURES POSITION
a.	You exercise 7 October 100 calls	+7 December futures
b.	You are assigned on 4 February 40 puts	+ 4 March futures
c.	You exercise 11 September 250 puts	−11 September futures
d.	You are assigned on 20 May 75 calls	−20 June futures

For serial options on futures where there is no futures month corresponding to the option expiration month, the underlying contract is the nearest listed futures month beyond the option expiration.

e.

ACTION	FUTURES POSITION	CASH FLOW
you exercise 26 March 1350 calls	**+26 March futures**	**+150,280**
you exercise 17 April 1425 puts	**−17 June futures**	**+137,360**
you are assigned 9 April 1375 calls	**−9 June futures**	**−17,280**
you are assigned on 40 February 1400 puts	**+40 March futures**	**−168,800**
totals	**+66 March futures**	**+101,560**
	−26 June futures	

5.

	ACTION	INDEX PRICE	INDEX POINT VALUE	UNDERLYING POSITION	CASH FLOW
a.	you exercise 10 March 5000 calls	5,353.63	10	**none**	**+35,363,00**
b.	you are assigned 7 June 2400 puts	2,318.35	500	**none**	**−42,325.00**
c.	you exercise on 21 September 1850 puts	1,832.48	250	**none**	**+4,380.00**
d.	you are assigned on 36 December 3900 calls	4,254.11	100	**none**	**−1,274,796.00**

Exercise or assignment of a cash index option results in no underlying position. There is only a cash payment equal to the difference between the exercise price and index price, multiplied by the index point value.

6.

	OPTION	OPTION PRICE	UNDERLYING PRICE	INTRINSIC VALUE	TIME VALUE
a.	January 90 call	4.75	85.00	**0**	**4.75**
b.	March 75 put	4.70	71.60	**3.40**	**1.30**
c.	May 125 call	22.25	147.25	**22.25**	**0**
d.	July 40 put	1.35	45.65	**0**	**1.35**
e.	September 1,300 call	31.80	1,303.25	**3.25**	**28.55**

(continued on next page)

	OPTION	OPTION PRICE	UNDERLYING PRICE	INTRINSIC VALUE	TIME VALUE
f.	November 600 put	71.50	528.50	**71.50**	**0**
g.	February 2500 call	67.25	2,491.00	**0**	**67.25**
h.	April 250 put	20.15	231.15	**18.85**	**1.20**
i.	June 15 call	.95	15.10	**.10**	**.85**
j.	August 5500 put	650.00	4,850.00	**650.00**	**0**
k.	October 32.50 call	1.10	33.45	**.95**	**.15**
l.	December 100 put	9.80	93.90	**6.10**	**3.70**

7.

	UNDERLYING PRICE	EXERCISE PRICE	OPTION TYPE	OPTION PRICE	INTRINSIC VALUE	TIME VALUE
a.	**74.10**	70	call	6.75	4.10	**2.65**
b.	78.15	**75**	call	4.55	**3.15**	1.40
c.	73.65	80	**put**	**7.10**	6.35	.75
d.	64.90	**70**	put	6.00	5.10	**.90**
e.	**71.50**	60	call	**12.00**	11.50	.50
f.	68.50	65	put	2.50	**0**	**2.50**
g.	891.20	**875**	call	22.45	**16.20**	6.25
h.	817.90	825	**put**	**17.10**	7.10	10.00
i.	**876.25**	850	call	33.75	**26.25**	7.50
j.	866.25	**900**	put	**36.85**	33.75	3.10
k.	796.40	800	**call**	12.75	0	**12.75**
l.	**875.00**	925	put	**52.50**	50.00	2.50

8.

	OPTION	UNDERLYING PRICE	IN-THE-MONEY OR OUT-OF-THE-MONEY	BY HOW MUCH?
a.	March 75 call	81.50	in-the-money	6.50
b.	July 2300 put	2,475.00	out-of-the-money	175.00
c.	November 650 call	648.00	out-of-the-money	2.00
d.	February 17.50 put	17.35	in-the-money	.15
e.	June 130 call	165.25	in-the-money	35.25
f.	October 117 put	117.66	out-of-the-money	.66

9. Options are currently listed for trading at the following exercise prices:

45, 50, 55, 60, 65, 70, 75

	UNDERLYING PRICE	EXERCISE PRICE THAT IS CLOSEST TO AT-THE-MONEY	EXERCISE PRICES FOR WHICH CALLS ARE IN-THE-MONEY	EXERCISE PRICES FOR WHICH PUTS ARE IN-THE-MONEY
a.	55.00	55	45 and 50	60, 65, 70, 75
b.	64.50	65	45, 50, 55, 60	65, 70, 75
c.	51.75	50	45, 50	55, 60, 65, 70, 75
d.	67.00	65	45, 50, 55, 60, 65	70, 75

10. Underlying price = 101.90

OPTION	CALL PRICE	CALL INTRINSIC VALUE	CALL TIME VALUE	PUT PRICE	PUT INTRINSIC VALUE	PUT TIME VALUE
April 80	23.00	21.90	1.10	.50	0	.50
April 85	18.25	16.90	1.35	.70	0	.70
April 90	13.60	11.90	1.70	1.20	0	1.20
April 95	9.65	6.90	2.75	2.15	0	2.15
April 100	6.15	1.90	4.25	3.65	0	3.65
April 105	3.60	0	3.60	6.10	3.10	3.00
April 110	2.00	0	2.00	9.50	8.10	1.40

(continued on next page)

OPTION	CALL PRICE	CALL INTRINSIC VALUE	CALL TIME VALUE	PUT PRICE	PUT INTRINSIC VALUE	PUT TIME VALUE
April 115	1.05	0	1.05	13.75	13.10	.65
April 120	.65	0	.65	18.25	18.10	.15
May 80	24.25	21.90	2.35	1.25	0	1.25
May 85	19.80	16.90	2.90	1.80	0	1.80
May 90	15.75	11.90	3.85	2.70	0	2.70
May 95	12.25	6.90	5.35	4.00	0	4.00
May 100	9.10	1.90	7.20	6.00	0	6.00
May 105	6.50	0	6.50	8.50	3.10	5.40
May 110	4.50	0	4.50	11.50	8.10	3.40
May 115	3.15	0	3.15	15.15	13.10	2.05
May 120	2.10	0	2.10	19.15	18.10	1.05

The option that is closest to at-the-money (the option whose exercise price is closest to the current underlying price) carries the greatest amount of time value.

The option that is furthest from at-the-money (the option whose exercise price is furthest from the current underlying price) carries the least amount of time value.

CHAPTER 4

Expiration Profit and Loss

1.

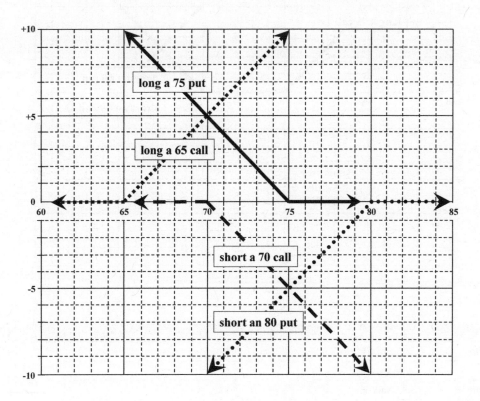

2.

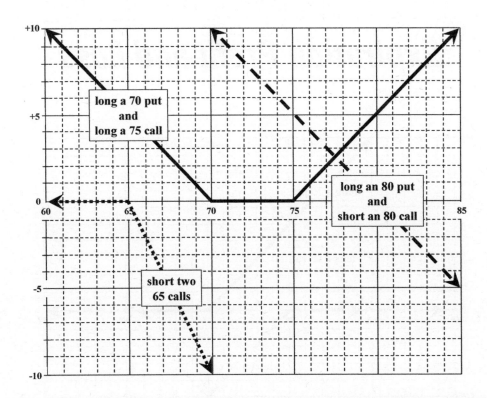

long a 70 put
and
long a 75 call

long an 80 put
and
short an 80 call

short two
65 calls

3.

	POSITION	UNDERLYING PRICE	SLOPE	SKETCH
a.	long 2 January 70 calls	below 70	0	
		above 70	+2	
b.	short 3 February 65 puts	below 65	+3	
		above 65	0	

(continued on next page)

	POSITION	UNDERLYING PRICE	SLOPE	SKETCH
c.	long 4 March 75 puts	below 75	−4	
		above 75	0	
d.	short 9 April 60 calls	below 60	0	
		above 60	−9	
e.	long 2 May 70 calls	below 70	−2	
	long 2 May 70 puts	above 70	+2	
f.	long 2 June 70 calls	below 65	+2	
	short 2 June 65 puts	between 65 and 70	0	
		above 70	+2	
g.	short 5 July 75 calls	below 75	−5	
	long 5 July 75 puts	above 75	−5	
h.	short 10 August 70 calls	below 70	+5	
	long 5 underlying contracts	above 70	−5	
i.	long 3 September 70 calls	below 65	0	
	short 3 September 65 puts	between 65 and 70	−3	
	short 3 underlying contracts	above 70	0	
j.	short 4 October 60 calls	below 60	+7	
	short 3 October 75 puts	between 60 and 75	+3	
	long 4 underlying contracts	above 75	0	
k.	long 5 November 65 calls	below 65	−1	
	short 8 November 65 puts	between 65 and 70	−4	
	long 4 November 70 calls	between 70 and 75	0	
	long 9 November 75 puts	above 75	+9	
l.	long 7 December 60 puts	below 60	−4	
	short 3 December 65 calls	between 60 and 65	+3	
	short 8 December 70 puts	between 65 and 70	0	
	short 5 underlying contracts	above 70	−8	

4. underlying price = 72.00

MARCH OPTIONS	65	70	75	80
calls	9.00	5.50	3.00	1.50
puts	1.00	2.50	4.75	8.25

a. long a March 70 call: **breakeven = 75.50**

b. short a March 65 put: **breakeven = 64.00**

c. long a March 75 put: **breakeven = 70.25**

d. short a March 80 call: **breakeven = 81.50**

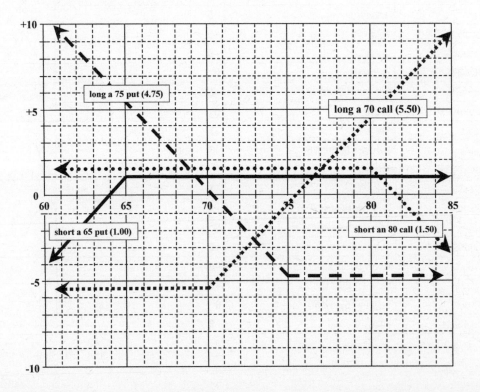

e. long a March 70 call and short a March 80 call: **breakeven = 74.00**

f. long a March 80 put and short 2 March 70 puts: **breakevens = 63.25; 76.75**

g. short a March 70 call and long a March 70 put: **breakevens = 73.00**

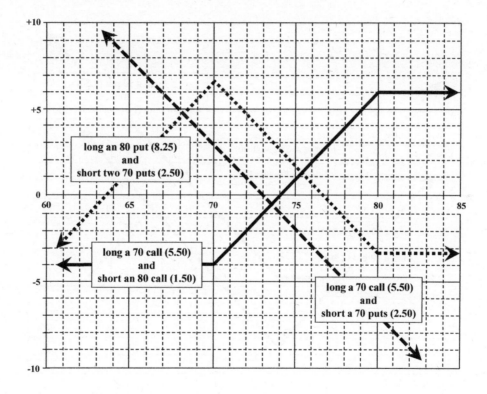

h. long a March 70 put and long an underlying contract: **breakeven = 74.50**

i. long a March 65 put and short a March 75 call: **breakeven = 77.00**

j. long a March 70 call and long a March 70 put: **breakevens = 62.00; 78.00**

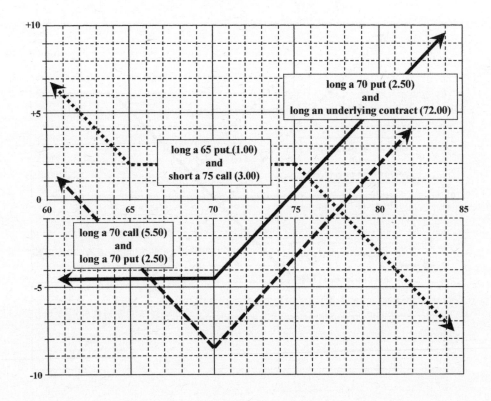

5. a.

CONTRACT POSITION	CONTRACT PRICE	CONTRACT VALUE AT 70.00	TOTAL CONTRACT PROFIT OR LOSS
−4 March 70 calls	6.00	0	**+24.00**
−5 March 70 puts	3.25	0	**+16.25**
+6 March 75 calls	4.50	0	**−27.00**
+8 March 75 puts	2.00	**5.00**	**+24.00**
+6 underlying contracts	73.00	**70.00**	**−18.00**
Total P&L at 70.00			**+19.25**

b.

	PRICE	EXPIRATION SLOPE
i.	below 70	**+3**
ii.	between 70 and 75	**−6**
iii.	above 75	**+8**

c.

	UNDERLYING PRICE	PROFIT OR LOSS AT EXPIRATION
i.	65.00	$19.25 - (3 \times 5.00) =$ **+4.25**
ii.	75.00	$19.25 - (6 \times 5.00) =$ **−10.75**
iii.	85.00	$-19.25 - (6 \times 5.00) + (8 \times 10.00) =$ **+69.75**

d. $65.00 - (4.25 / 3) \approx$ **63.58**

$70.00 + (19.25 / 6) \approx$ **73.21**

$75.00 + (10.75 / 8) \approx$ **76.34**

e. On the following grid, draw the value of your position at expiration.

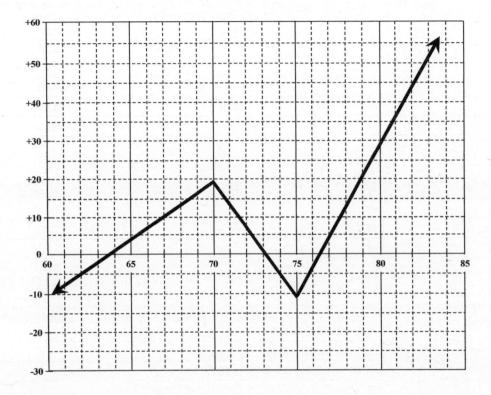

| CHAPTER 5 |

Theoretical Evaluation

1. **a.** forward price = **110.00**

    b.

	OPTION	EXPECTED VALUE
i.	70 call	$(.20 \times 20) + (.30 \times 40) + (.20 \times 60) + (.10 \times 80) + (.05 \times 100) = \mathbf{41.00}$
ii.	70 put	$(.05 \times 20) = \mathbf{1.00}$
iii.	110 call	$(.20 \times 20) + (.10 \times 40) + (.05 \times 60) = \mathbf{11.00}$
iv.	110 put	$(.20 \times 20) + (.10 \times 40) + (.05 \times 60) = \mathbf{11.00}$
v.	135 call	$(.10 \times 15) + (.05 \times 35) = \mathbf{3.25}$
vi.	135 put	$(.20 \times 5) + (.30 \times 25) + (.20 \times 45) + (.10 \times 65) + (.05 \times 85) = \mathbf{28.25}$

    c. call expected value – put expected value = forward price – exercise price
    (They differ by intrinsic value against the forward price.)

    d.

	OPTION	THEORETICAL VALUE
i.	70 call	$41.00 / (1+.06 \times 3/12) = \mathbf{4.39}$
ii.	70 put	$1.00 / (1+.06 \times 3/12) = \mathbf{.99}$
iii.	110 call	$11.00 / (1+.06 \times 3/12) = \mathbf{10.84}$
iv.	110 put	$11.00 / (1+.06 \times 3/12) = \mathbf{10.84}$
v.	135 call	$3.25 / (1+.06 \times 3/12) = \mathbf{3.20}$
vi.	135 put	$28.25 / (1+.06 \times 3/12) = \mathbf{27.83}$

e. $F = S \times (1 + r \times t) - D$

$S = (F + D) / (1 + r \times t)$

$(110.00 + .75) / (1 + .06 \times 3/12) = \textbf{109.11}$

2. **a.** $F = S \times (1 + rt) = 72.50 \times (1 + .08 \times 6/12) = \textbf{75.40}$

   b.

F − 2I	F − I	F	F + I	F + 2I
65.40	**70.40**	**75.40**	**80.40**	**85.40**

   c. $(.08 \times 65.40) + (.18 \times 70.40) + (.34 \times 75.40) + (.26 \times 80.40) + (.14 \times 85.40) = \textbf{76.40}$

   d. Buy the stock and hold it for six months. Buying and holding the stock will cost 75.40, but the average price of the stock in six months will be 76.40. You will show an average profit of 1.00.

   e.

i.	70 call	expected value = $(.18 \times .40) + (.34 \times 5.40) + (.26 \times 10.40) + (.14 \times 15.40) = \textbf{6.77}$ theoretical value = $6.77 / (1 + .08 \times 6/12) = \textbf{6.51}$
ii.	70 put	expected value = $(.08 \times 4.60) = \textbf{.37}$ theoretical value = $.37 / (1 + .08 \times 6/12) = \textbf{.35}$
iii.	80 call	expected value = $(.26 \times .40) + (.14 \times 5.40) = \textbf{.86}$ theoretical value = $.86 / (1 + .08 \times 6/12) = \textbf{.83}$
iv.	80 put	expected value = $(.34 \times 4.60) + (.18 \times 9.60) + (.08 \times 14.60) = \textbf{4.46}$ theoretical value = $4.46 / (1 + .08 \times 6/12) = \textbf{4.29}$

3. a. The relationship does not hold true. The relationship is only true if the forward price and average price for the underlying contract (the expected value for the underlying contract) are equal.

The relationship is now:

> call expected value – put expected value = underlying expected value – exercise price.

For no arbitrage opportunity to exist, the forward price and expected value must be equal.

b. $F = S \times (1 + rt)$

$r = (F/S - 1) / t$

$(76.40/72.50 - 1) / (6/12) = \mathbf{10.76\%}$

c.

F – 2I	F – I	F	F + I	F + 2I
55.40	**65.40**	**75.40**	**85.40**	**95.40**

d. $(.08 \times 55.40) + (.18 \times 65.40) + (.34 \times 75.40) + (.26 \times 85.40) + (.14 \times 95.40) = \mathbf{77.40}$

e.

i.	70 call	expected value = $(.34 \times 5.40) + (.26 \times 15.40) + (.14 \times 25.40) = \mathbf{9.40}$ theoretical value = $9.40 / (1 + .08 \times 6/12) = \mathbf{9.04}$
ii.	70 put	expected value = $(.18 \times 4.60) + (.08 \times 14.60) = \mathbf{2.00}$ theoretical value = $.37 / (1 + .08 \times 6/12) = \mathbf{1.92}$
iii.	80 call	expected value = $(.26 \times 5.40) + (.14 \times 15.40) = \mathbf{3.56}$ theoretical value = $3.56 / (1 + .08 \times 6/12) = \mathbf{3.42}$
iv.	80 put	expected value = $(.34 \times 4.60) + (.18 \times 14.60) + (.08 \times 24.60) = \mathbf{6.16}$ theoretical value = $6.16 / (1 + .08 \times 6/12) = \mathbf{5.92}$

f. The relationship is still the same:

> call expected value – put expected value = underlying expected value – exercise price.

This relationship is commonly referred to as *put-call parity*.

| CHAPTER 6 |

Volatility

1. a. contract price = 78.00

VOLATILITY	20%	30%	40%	50%
daily standard deviation	.98	1.46	1.95	2.44
weekly standard deviation	2.17	3.25	4.33	5.42

b. contract price = 1,325.00

VOLATILITY	10%	15%	20%	25%
daily standard deviation	8.28	12.42	16.56	20.70
weekly standard deviation	18.40	27.60	36.81	46.01

c. contract price = 1.6270

VOLATILITY	8%	10%	12%	14%
daily standard deviation	.0081	.0102	.0122	.0142
weekly standard deviation	.0181	.0226	.0271	.0316

d. contract price = 669.00

VOLATILITY	15%	23%	31%	39%
daily standard deviation	6.27	9.62	12.96	16.31
weekly standard deviation	13.94	21.37	28.80	36.24

e. contract price = 3,187.00

VOLATILITY	13%	17%	21%	25%
daily standard deviation	25.89	33.86	41.83	49.80
weekly standard deviation	57.54	75.25	92.95	110.66

2.

	FUTURES PRICE	VOLATILITY	TIME PERIOD	DOWN ONE ST. DEV.	UP ONE ST. DEV.	DOWN TWO ST. DEVS.	UP TWO ST. DEVS.
a.	226.00	21%	14 weeks	201.37	250.63	176.75	275.25
b.	1,869.00	14%	11 months	1,618.48	2,119.52	1,367.96	2,370.04
c.	103.82	9.5%	116 days	98.26	109.38	92.70	114.94
d.	16.97	38%	5 months	12.81	21.13	8.64	25.30
e.	9,623	18.25%	23 weeks	8,455	10,791	7,287	11,959

3.

	FUTURES PRICE	VOLATILITY	TIME PERIOD	DOWN ONE ST. DEV.	UP ONE ST. DEV.	DOWN TWO ST. DEVS.	UP TWO ST. DEVS.
a.	226.00	21%	14 weeks	202.67	252.02	181.75	281.03
b.	1,869.00	14%	11 months	1,634.54	2,137.09	1,429.50	2,443.63
c.	103.82	9.5%	116 days	98.41	109.53	93.27	115.56
d.	16.97	38%	5 months	13.28	21.69	10.39	27.72
e.	9,623	18.25%	23 weeks	8,523	10,865	7,549	12,267

Using exponential calculations, upward moves are larger and downward moves are smaller than if we use simple calculations.

4. a. forward price = $104.75 \times (1 + .0619 \times 192/365) - 2.28 = \textbf{105.88}$

$105.88 \times [1 \pm .2742 \times \sqrt{(192/365)}] = \textbf{84.82 to 126.94}$ ($\pm$ 1 standard deviation)

$105.88 \times [1 \pm 2 \times .2742 \times \sqrt{(192/365)}] = \textbf{63.77 to 147.99}$ ($\pm$ 2 standard deviations)

b. forward price = 104.75 × exp(.0619 × 192/365) − 2.28 × exp(.0619 × (192 − 43)/365) = **105.88**
(coincidentally, the same forward price as in part a)

105.88 × [1 ± .2742 × $\sqrt{(192/365)}$] = **86.79 to 129.18** (± 1 standard deviation)

105.88 × [1± 2 × .2742 × $\sqrt{(192/365)}$] = **71.13 to 157.60** (± 2 standard deviations)

5. a.

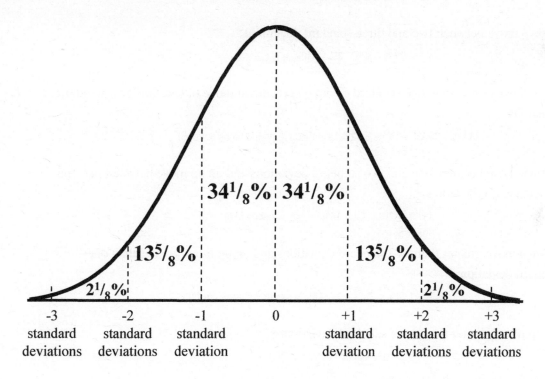

b. **i.** An up move less than two standard deviations:

$$34\tfrac{1}{8}\% + 13\tfrac{5}{8}\% = \mathbf{47\tfrac{3}{4}\%} \text{ (slightly less than 1 chance in 2)}$$

ii. An up or down move between one and two standard deviations:

$$2 \times 13\tfrac{5}{8}\% = \mathbf{27\tfrac{1}{4}\%} \text{ (slightly more than 1 chance in 4)}$$

iii. A down move between two and three standard deviations:

$$2\tfrac{1}{8}\% - \tfrac{1}{8}\% = \mathbf{2\%} \text{ (1 chance in 50)}$$

iv. An up move of less than one standard deviation or a down move of less than two standard deviations:

$$34\tfrac{1}{4}\% + 34\tfrac{1}{4}\% + 13\tfrac{1}{2}\% = \mathbf{82\%} \text{ (slightly more than 4 times out of 5)}$$

v. A down move between one and two standard deviations and an up move between two and three standard deviations:

$$13\tfrac{5}{8}\% + 2\tfrac{1}{8}\% - \tfrac{1}{8} = \mathbf{16\%} \text{ (about 1 chance in 6)}$$

vi. A down move greater than two standard deviations and an up move greater than one standard deviation:

$$\tfrac{1}{8} + 2\tfrac{1}{8}\% + 13\tfrac{5}{8}\% + 2\tfrac{1}{8}\% + \tfrac{1}{8} = \mathbf{18\tfrac{1}{8}\%} \text{ (about 2 chances in 11)}$$

vii. An up move greater than three standard deviations:

$$\mathbf{\tfrac{1}{8}\%} \text{ (about 1 chance in 800)}$$

6. a. If the underlying contract price is close to 100, each price move can be interpreted as an approximate percentage move:

DAY 1	+.75%
DAY 2	−2.40%
DAY 3	+1.75%
DAY 4	+.40%
DAY 5	+3.20%
DAY 6	−1.55%
DAY 7	−1.00%
DAY 8	+.15%
DAY 9	+1.40%
DAY 10	−.55%

At a volatility of 20% a daily standard deviation is approximately 20%/16 = 1¼%, or about 1.25. You would therefore expect to see a move greater than 1.25 (greater than one standard deviation) about one time in three, or about three times in 10 days. But there were actually five days when the price change was greater than 1.25. So a volatility of 20% seems too low.

b. We might note that the three largest price changes were 1.75 or more, while the seven smallest price changes were 1.55 or less. One standard deviation is probably somewhere between these two values. Taking the midpoint of 1.65, we can estimate that a one-standard-deviation price change is probably close to 1.65%. The annualized volatility for the 10-day period should therefore be close to 1.65% × 16 = 26.40%. (The actual value is approximately 26.60%.)

CHAPTER 7

Risk Measurement

1.

RISK MEASURE	DEFINITION
1. theta	**A.** the sensitivity of an option's theoretical value to a change in volatility
2. gamma	**B.** The sensitivity of an option's theoretical value to a change in the underlying price
3. rho	**C.** The sensitivity of an option's delta to a change in the underlying price
4. vega	**D.** The sensitivity of an option's theoretical value to a change in interest rates
5. delta	**E.** The sensitivity of an option's theoretical value to the passage of time

1. E; 2. C; 3. D; 4. A; 5. B

2. The delta can be used to estimate the effect of a dividend change.

3.

	CURRENT OPTION VALUE	DELTA (WHOLE NUMBER FORMAT)	UNDERLYING PRICE CHANGE	NEW OPTION VALUE
a.	10.25	60	+.40	$10.25 + (.60 \times .40) = \mathbf{10.49}$
b.	24.60	−44	−5.20	$24.60 + (−.44 \times −5.20) = \mathbf{26.89}$
c.	5.41	27	−2.30	$5.41 + (.27 \times −2.30) = \mathbf{4.79}$
d.	51.40	−15	+13.68	$51.40 + (−.15 \times 13.68) = \mathbf{49.35}$
e.	1.24	72	+.18	$1.24 + (.72 \times .18) = \mathbf{1.37}$
f.	8.90	−85	−5.25	$8.90 + (−.85 \times −5.25) = \mathbf{13.36}$

Positive deltas are calls; negative deltas are puts.

4.

	CURRENT OPTION VALUE	DELTA	GAMMA	UNDERLYING PRICE CHANGE	NEW OPTION DELTA	NEW OPTION VALUE
a.	4.58	57	4	+3.00	$57 + (3 \times 4) = \textbf{69}$	$4.58 + 3 \times (.57 + .69)/2 = \textbf{6.47}$
b.	1.70	−39	7	−.94	$-39 - (.94 \times 7) = \textbf{−45.58}$	$1.70 - .94 \times (-.39 - .4558)/2 = \textbf{2.10}$
c.	4.94	28	1.1	−8.50	$28 - (8.50 \times 1.1) = \textbf{18.65}$	$4.94 - 8.50 \times (.28 + .1865)/2 = \textbf{2.96}$
d.	10.09	−83	2.8	−6.75	$-83 - (6.75 \times 2.8) = -101.9\ \textbf{(−100)}$	$10.09 - 6.75 \times (-.83 - 1.00)/2 = \textbf{16.27}$
e.	.58	21	6.5	−3.70	$21 - (3.70 \times 6.5) = -3.05\ \textbf{(0)}$	$.58 - 3.70 \times (.21 + 0)/2 = \textbf{.19}$
f.	3.95	−12	.3	+18.20	$-12 + (18.20 \times .3) = \textbf{−6.54}$	$3.95 + 18.20 \times (-.12 - .0654)/2 = \textbf{2.26}$

Regardless of the gamma values, the delta can never be less than zero, nor more than 100 for calls or −100 for puts.

5.

	OPTION VALUE	RISK MEASURE	CHANGE IN MARKET CONDITIONS	NEW OPTION VALUE
a.	5.18	theta = −.095	2 days pass	$5.18 - (2 \times .095) = \textbf{4.99}$
b.	.67	vega = .047	volatility rises 3.2%	$.67 + (3.2 \times .047) = \textbf{.82}$
c.	22.75	rho = −.177	interest rates rise 2.90%	$22.75 - (.177 \times 2.90) = \textbf{22.24}$
d.	1.64	theta = −.024	13 days pass	$1.64 - (13 \times .024) = \textbf{1.33}$
e.	12.10	vega = .232	volatility falls 5.6%	$12.10 - (5.6 \times .232) = \textbf{10.80}$
f.	3.99	rho = .088	interest rates fall 1.67%	$3.99 - (1.67 \times .088) = \textbf{3.84}$

6. a. average delta = 62 − (3.28 × 4.4) / 2 = **54.8**

change due to stock price = −3.28 × .548 = **−1.80**

change due to implied volatility = 2.6 × .13 = **.34**

new option price = 4.55 −1.80 +.34 = **3.09**

b. change due to the passage of time = 6 × −.199 = **−1.19**

change due to interest rates = −1.20 × −.135 = + **.16**

new option price = 8.87 − 1.19 +.16 = **7.84**

c. change due to the passage of time = 4 × −.027 = **−.11**

change due to implied volatility = −1.75 × .217 = **−.38**

change due to interest rates = .75 × .142 = **+.11**

change due to dividend = .43 × −.37 = **−.16**

new option price = 4.73 − .11 − .38 + .11 − .16 = **4.19**

7. a. A position with a positive delta wants **the underlying price to rise.**

b. A position with a negative gamma wants **the underlying contract to sit still, or move very slowly.**

c. A position with a negative rho wants **interest rates to fall.**

d. A position with a positive vega wants **implied volatility to rise.**

e. A position with a positive gamma wants **the underlying contract to make a big move, or move very quickly.**

f. A position with a positive delta and negative gamma wants **the underlying contract to move up slowly.**

8. **a.** If the underlying price remains unchanged, as time passes a position with a negative theta will **decline in value.**

   b. If the underlying price remains unchanged, as time passes a position with a positive gamma will **decline in value.**

   c. If interest rates fall, a position with a negative rho will **increase in value.**

   d. If implied volatility falls, a position with a negative vega will **increase in value.**

   e. If the underlying price makes a large move, a position with a positive theta will **decline in value.**

   f. If the underlying price makes a large move, a position with a positive gamma will **increase in value.**

9. **a.** A trader who buys calls has a **short** theta position.

   b. A trader who sells puts has a **long** delta position

   c. A trader who sells puts has a **short** gamma position.

   d. A trader who sells calls has a **short** vega position.

   e. A trader who buys stock option puts has a **short** rho position.

   f. A trader who sells puts has a **long** theta position.

   g. A trader who buys puts has a **long** vega position.

   h. A trader who sells stock option calls has a **short** rho position.

   i. A trader who buys calls has a **long** gamma position.

10.

RISK MEASURES	FAVORABLE CHANGES IN MARKET CONDITIONS
1. positive delta negative gamma negative vega positive rho	**A** swift upward price move indifferent to changes in implied volatility falling interest rates
2. zero delta positive gamma negative vega negative rho	**B** downward price movement indifferent to changes in implied volatility indifferent to changes in interest rates
3. negative delta negative gamma positive vega positive rho	**C** slow upward price movement falling implied volatility rising interest rates
4. positive delta positive gamma zero vega negative rho	**D** swift price move in either direction falling implied volatility falling interest rates
5. negative delta zero gamma zero vega zero rho	**E** slow downward price movement rising implied volatility rising interest rates

1. C; 2. D; 3. E; 4. A; 5. B

11. a. i. delta position:

$$(5 \times 79) - (6 \times 52) - (14 \times 26) + (8 \times 21) + (11 \times 48) - (6 \times 74) + (3 \times 100) = \mathbf{+271}$$

ii. gamma position:

$$(5 \times 4.2) - (6 \times 5.8) - (14 \times 4.7) - (8 \times 4.2) - (11 \times 5.8) + (6 \times 4.7) = \mathbf{-148.8}$$

iii. theta position:

$$(5 \times -.0190) - (6 \times -.0205) - (14 \times -0152) - (8 \times -.0084) - (11 \times -.0092) + (6 \times -.0030) = \textbf{+.3912}$$

iv. vega position:

$$(5 \times .010) - (6 \times .137) - (14 \times .112) - (8 \times .010) - (11 \times .137) + (6 \times .112) = \textbf{-3.525}$$

v. rho position:

$$(5 \times .121) - (6 \times .083) - (14 \times .043) - (8 \times -.039) - (11 \times -.089) + (6 \times -.142) = \textbf{-.056}$$

b. a slow upward move in the underlying price
falling implied volatility
falling interest rates

c. change due to the underlying price:

average delta position = +271 − (148.8 × 3.50)/2 = 10.6

.106 × 3.50 = **+.37**

change due to the passage of time: 3 × .3912 = **+1.17**

change due to volatility: 2.40 × −3.525 = **−8.46**

change due to interest rates: −.50 × −.056 = **+.03**

new theoretical edge: +4.65 +.37 +1.17 − 8.46 +.03 = **−2.24**

Now you expect to show a loss of 2.24 on the position.

CHAPTER 8

Delta Neutral Positions and Dynamic Hedging

1. **a.** delta position = $25 \times 41 = \mathbf{1{,}025}$

i.	underlying contract	1,025/100 = 10.25	**sell 10**
ii.	July 90 call	1,025/18 = 56.94	**sell 57**
iii.	July 80 put	1,025/−59 = −17.37	**buy 17**

   b. delta position = $-50 \times -30 = \mathbf{+1{,}500}$

i.	July 70 call	1,500/70 = 21.43	**sell 21**
ii.	July 80 put	1,500/−59 = −25.43	**buy 25**
iii.	July 90 put	1,500/−82 = −18.29	**buy 18**

   c. delta position = $-15 \times 100 = \mathbf{-1{,}500}$

   $-1{,}500/2 = \mathbf{-750}$

−750/−59 = 12.71	**sell 13 July 80 puts**
−750/18 = −41.67	**buy 42 July 90 calls**

2. **a.** long 10 calls

CURRENT OPTION DELTA	CURRENT TOTAL DELTA POSITION	UNDERLYING CONTRACTS TO BUY OR SELL
70	+700	sell 7
50	−200	buy 2
40	−100	buy 1
80	+400	sell 4

b. short 30 calls

OPTION DELTA	DELTA POSITION	UNDERLYING CONTRACTS TO BUY OR SELL
28	−840	buy 8
40	−400	buy 4
63	−690	buy 7
52	+340	sell 3

c. long 62 puts

OPTION DELTA	CURRENT TOTAL DELTA POSITION	UNDERLYING CONTRACTS TO BUY OR SELL
−65	−4,030	buy 40
−71	−402	buy 4
−33	−2,354	sell 24
−49	−1,038	buy 10

d. short 44 puts

OPTION DELTA	CURRENT TOTAL DELTA POSITION	UNDERLYING CONTRACTS TO BUY OR SELL
−95	+4,180	sell 42
−77	−812	buy 8
−40	−1,640	buy 16
0	−1,800	buy 18

3. a. 55 call

UNDERLYING PRICE	DELTA	HEDGE	CASH FLOW	TOTAL HEDGE
53.70	45	sell .45	+.45 × 53.70 = +24.17	−.45
55.70	57	sell .12	+.12 × 55.70 = +6.68	−.57
53.40	40	buy .17	−.17 × 53.40 = −9.08	−.40
57.10	69	sell .29	+.29 × 57.10 = +16.56	−.69
55.00	51	buy .18	−.18 × 55.00 = −9.90	−.51
51.50		buy .51	−.51 × 51.50 = −26.27	0

Dynamic hedge cash flow: +24.17 + 6.68 − 9.08 + 16.56 − 9.90 − 26.27 = +2.16

Intrinsic value at expiration = 0

Value of the 55 call = 2.16 + 0 = **2.16**

b. 70 put

UNDERLYING PRICE	DELTA	HEDGE	CASH FLOW	TOTAL HEDGE
68.42	−65	buy .65	−.65 × 68.42 = −44.47	+.65
69.71	−52	sell .13	+.13 × 69.71 = +9.06	+.52
71.29	−33	sell .19	+.19 × 71.29 = +13.55	+.33
70.19	−46	buy .13	−.13 × 70.19 = −9.12	+.46
71.02	−28	sell .18	+.18 × 71.02 = +12.78	+.28
68.51		sell .28	+.28 × 68.51 = +19.18	0

Dynamic hedge cash flow: −44.47 + 9.06 + 13.55 − 9.12 + 12.78 + 19.18 = +.98

Intrinsic value at expiration = 70.00 − 68.51 = 1.49

Value of the 70 put = .98 + 1.49 = **2.47**

CHAPTER 9

The Dynamics of Risk

1. **a.** The underlying price changes, but all other market conditions remain unchanged, which option's price will change the most?

   i. **a 1-month 75 call**
   a 1-month 80 call

   ii. a 1-month 75 put
   a 1-month 80 put

   iii. **a 1-month 80 put**
   a 3-month 80 put

   b. If the underlying price changes, but all other market conditions remain unchanged, which option's delta will change the most?

   i. **a 1-month 75 call**
   a 1-month 80 call

   ii. **a 1-month 75 call**
   a 3-month 75 call

   iii. a 1-month 65 put
   a 3-month 65 put

   c. If the implied volatility changes by the same amount for all options, but all other market conditions remain unchanged, which option's price will change the most?

   i. a 3-month 70 put
   a 3-month 75 put

   ii. a 1-month 75 put
   a 3-month 75 put

   iii. a 1-month 85 call
   a 3-month 85 call

   d. If two weeks pass with no change in the price of the underlying contract, but all other market conditions remain unchanged, which option's price will change the most?

   i. a 1-month 70 call
   a 1-month 75 call

   ii. **a 1-month 75 call**
   a 3-month 75 call

   iii. a 1-month 65 put
   a 3-month 65 put

e. If the underlying contract is stock, and interest rates change by the same amount for all expiration months, but all other market conditions remain unchanged, which option's price will change the most?

    i. **a 3-month 70 call**   **ii.** a 1-month 80 call   **iii.** a 1-month 70 put

       a 3-month 75 call   **a 3-month 80 call**   **a 1-month 75 put**

f. If the underlying contract is a stock which is expected to pay a dividend in two months, if the dividend is changed but all other market conditions remain unchanged, which option's price will change the most?

    i. **a 3-month 70 call**   **ii.** a 1-month 80 call   **iii.** a 3-month 75 put

       a 3-month 75 call   **a 3-month 80 call**   **a 3-month 80 put**

2. a. The underlying price falls to 45

	DELTA	GAMMA	THETA	VEGA
40 call	–	+	+	+
50 call	–	–	–	–
60 call	–	–	–	–
40 put	+	+	+	+
50 put	+	–	–	–
60 put	+	–	–	–

b. The underlying price rises to 55

	DELTA	GAMMA	THETA	VEGA
40 call	+	−	−	−
50 call	+	−	−	−
60 call	+	+	+	+
40 put	−	−	−	−
50 put	−	−	−	−
60 put	−	+	+	+

c. Two weeks pass

	DELTA	GAMMA	THETA	VEGA
40 call	+	−	−	−
50 call	0	+	+	−
60 call	−	−	−	−
40 put	−	−	−	−
50 put	0	+	+	+
60 put	+	−	−	−

d. Volatility falls

	DELTA	GAMMA	THETA	VEGA
40 call	+	−	−	−
50 call	0	+	−	0
60 call	−	−	−	−
40 put	−	−	−	−
50 put	0	+	−	0
60 put	+	−	−	−

e. Volatility rises

	DELTA	GAMMA	THETA	VEGA
40 call	−	+	+	+
50 call	0	−	+	0
60 call	+	+	+	+
40 put	+	+	+	+
50 put	0	−	+	0
60 put	−	+	+	+

underlying stock price = 100

time to expiration = 3 months

Interest rate = 6.00%

volatility = 20%

	TH. VALUE	DELTA	GAMMA	THETA	VEGA	VANNA	CHARM	VOLGA	VEGA DECAY	SPEED	COLOR
90 call	11.86	.895	.018	−.0227	.091	−.010	.0009	.0066	−.0010	−.0025	0
100 call	4.74	.579	.039	−.0302	.195	−.002	−.0004	.0002	−.0010	−.0012	.0002
110 call	1.24	.225	.030	−.0200	.150	.013	−.0019	.0048	−.0015	.0020	0
90 put	.52	−.105	.018	−.0082	.091	−.010	.0009	.0066	−.0010	−.0025	0
100 put	3.25	−.421	.039	−.0140	.195	−.002	−.0004	.0002	−.0010	−.0012	.0002
110 put	9.61	−.775	.030	−.0022	.150	.013	−.0019	.0048	−.0015	.0020	0

3.

a.	If volatility falls to 18% what will be the new delta values of the 90 call and the 100 put?	using the vanna: 90 call delta = .895 − (2 × −.010) = **.915** 100 put delta = −.421 − (2 × −.002) = **−.417**
b.	If 10 days pass, what will be the new delta values of the 90 put and the 100 call?	using the charm: 90 put delta = −.105 + (10 × .0009) = **−.096** 100 call delta = .579 + (10 × −.0004) = **.575**
c.	If 10 days pass, what will be the new gamma values of the 90 call and the 100 put?	using the color: 90 call gamma = .018 + (10 × 0) = **.018** (no change) 100 put gamma = .039 + (10 × .0002) = **.041**
d.	If the underlying price falls to 96, what will be the new vega values of the 90 put and the 110 call?	using the vanna: 90 put vega = .091 − (4 × − .010) = **.131** 110 put vega = .150 − (4 × .013) = **.098**
e.	If the underlying price rises to 103, what will be the new theta values of the 90 call and the 110 put?	using the charm: 90 call theta = −.0227 + (3 × .0009) = **−.0200** 110 put theta = −.0022 + (3 × −.0019) = **−.0079**
f.	If ten days pass what will be the new vega values of the 100 call and 110 put?	using the vega decay: 100 call vega = .195 − (10 × .001) = **.185** 110 put vega = .150 − (10 × .0015) = **.135**
g.	If volatility rises to 25% what will be the new vega values of the 90 put and the 110 call?	using the volga: 90 put vega = .091 + (5 × .0066) = **.124** 110 call vega = .150 + (5 × .0048) = **.174**

The values in the above table were generated using the Black-Scholes model. For those who have a computer program that generates theoretical values and sensitivities, it may be useful to compare the given answers to computer-generated values. The given answers are only approximations since the higher order sensitivities also change as market conditions change.

4.

a.	If volatility rises to 25% what will be the approximate theoretical values of the 90 put and 100 call?	90 put average vega = (.091 + .124) / 2 = .1075 90 put theoretical value = .52 + (5 × .1075) = **1.06** 110 call average vega = (.150 + .174) / 2 = .162 110 call theoretical value = 1.24 + (5 × .162) = **2.05**
b.	If the stock price rises to 107 what will be the new gamma values of the 100 call and 110 put?	100 call gamma = .039 + (7 × −.0012) = **.0306** 110 put gamma = .030 + (7 × .002) = **.044**
c.	If the stock price rises to 107 what will be the new delta values of the 100 call and the 110 put?	100 call average gamma = (.039 + .0306) / 2 = .0348 100 call delta = .579 + (7 × .0348) = **.823** 110 put average gamma = (.030 + .044) / 2 = .037 110 put delta = −.775 + (7 × .037) = **−.516**
d.	If the stock price rises to 107 what will be the approximate theoretical values of the 100 call and the 110 put?	100 call average delta = (.579 + .823) / 2 = .701 100 call value = 4.74 + (7 × .701) = **9.65** 110 put average delta = (−.775 − .516) / 2 = −.6455 110 put value = 9.61 + (7 × −.6455) = **5.09**

5. **a.** percent change in the underlying price = (56.34 − 54.80) / 54.80 = .0281 (up 2.81%)

call price change = 5.25 × .0281 = .1475 (up 14.75%)

new call value = (1 + .1475) × 6.84 = **7.85**

put price change = −2.90 × .0281 = −.0815 (down 8.15%)

new put value = (1 − .0815) × 2.30 = **2.11**

b. call delta = (7.85 − 6.84) / (56.34 − 54.80) ≈ **.656 (65.6)**

put delta = (2.11 − 2.30)) / (56.34 − 54.80) ≈ **−.123 (−12.3)**

c. How does an option's elasticity relate to its delta?

elasticity = delta × (underlying price / option value)

6. **a.** delta at an underlying price of $75.00 = 48.0 + 1.5 \times 5.3 \approx 56.0$

average delta as the underlying price rises from 73.50 to $75.00 = (48.0+56.0) / 2 = 52.0$

theoretical value at an underlying price of $75.00 = 2.64 + 1.50 \times .52 = \mathbf{3.42}$

b. new option value = old option value + (change in underlying price × delta) + (change in underlying price^2 × gamma/2)

c. It may seem that a fair price for the 75 call is 3.42 with a delta of 56.

Suppose the market-maker sells the option at 3.42 and hedges the position by buying .56 of an underlying contract at a price of 75.00.

Given the actual market conditions (call value = 2.64, underlying price = 73.50) the market-maker's resulting P&L is $(3.42 - 2.64) - .56 \times (75.00 - 73.50) = -.06$

The fair value of the 75 call when tied to an underlying price of 75.00 must be .06 more than 3.42, or **3.48**.

d. When an option is tied to an underlying price different than the current underlying price, the option value changes not only because of the delta, but also because of the gamma. In order to determine a fair value for the "tied to" option, we must include the gamma portion of our calculation.

tied-to option value = theoretical value at the tied-to price + (change in underlying price^2 × gamma/2)

7. A—the price of the underlying stock rises

   B—volatility rises

   C—time passes

   D—interest rates rise

   E— the dividend is increased

   a. Which of the above changes in market conditions will cause the *delta* of an at-the-money call to increase? **A, D**

   b. Which of the above changes in market conditions will cause the *delta* of an out-of-the-money put to increase (become more negative)? **B, E**

   c. Which of the above changes in market conditions will cause the *gamma* of an at-the-money call to increase? **C**

   d. Which of the above changes in market conditions will cause the *gamma* of a deeply in-the-money put to increase? **A, B, D**

   e. Which of the above changes in market conditions will cause the *theta* of an at-the-money put to increase? **B, C**

   f. Which of the above changes in market conditions will cause the *vega* of an out-of-the-money call to increase? **A, B, D**

8. Futures price = 149.65

time to August expiration = 8 weeks

annual volatility = 24.20%

You have the following position:

August 140 puts

+30 August 160 calls

−15 August futures contracts

with the options having these risk sensitivities:

OPTION	DELTA	GAMMA	THETA	VEGA
August 140 put	−22.6	2.12	−.0381	.176
August 160 call	25.5	2.26	−.0407	.188

a.

DELTA	GAMMA	THETA	VEGA
−11.8	−.04	+.0018	+.008

b. The risk sensitivities seem so small that a trader might conclude that the position has essentially no risk.

c. Probably not. Focusing on the risk sensitivities solely under current market conditions may give a false impression of the actual risk. Even if the risk seems relatively small right now, it's important to consider what will happen if market conditions change, which they almost certainly will.

d. The delta, gamma, and vega will all become positive.

e. The delta will become positive.
The gamma and vega will become negative.

f. delta values will move toward 50
The total delta position will become positive.

g. delta values will move away from 50
The total delta position will become negative.

h. maximum downside delta = **+1,700** (–32 puts, –15 futures)

i. maximum upside delta = **+1,500** (+30 calls, –15 futures)

j. **2** the futures price falls slowly to 140 and implied volatility falls to 22.20%

4 the futures price falls quickly to 140 and implied volatility rises to 26.20%

3 the futures price rises slowly to 160 and implied volatility falls to 22.20%

1 the futures price rises quickly to 160 and implied volatility rises to 26.20%

k.

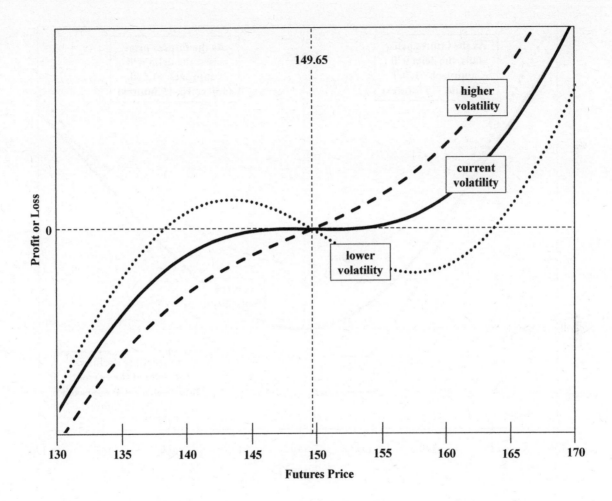

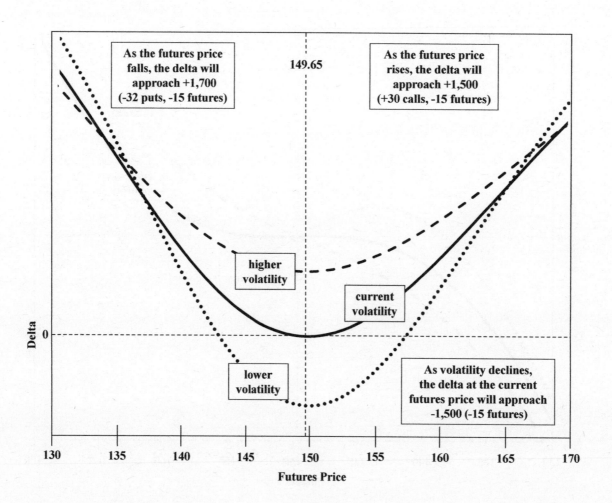

As the futures price falls, the delta will approach +1,700 (-32 puts, -15 futures)

149.65

As the futures price rises, the delta will approach +1,500 (+30 calls, -15 futures)

higher volatility

current volatility

lower volatility

As volatility declines, the delta at the current futures price will approach -1,500 (-15 futures)

Delta

0

Futures Price

130   135   140   145   150   155   160   165   170

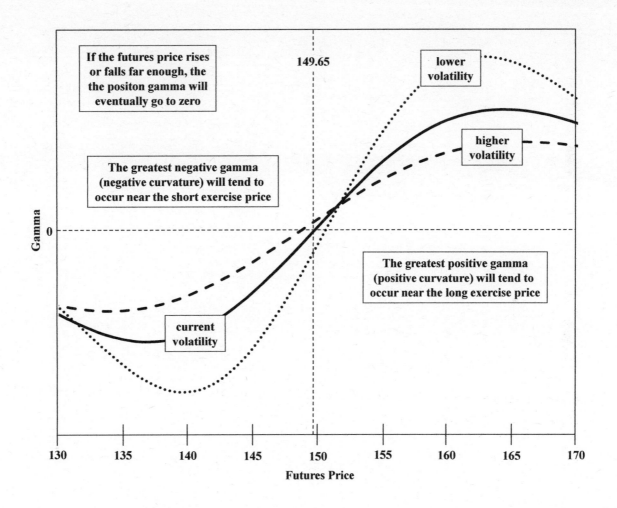

If the futures price rises
or falls far enough, the
the positon gamma will
eventually go to zero

149.65

lower
volatility

higher
volatility

The greatest negative gamma
(negative curvature) will tend to
occur near the short exercise price

0

The greatest positive gamma
(positive curvature) will tend to
occur near the long exercise price

current
volatility

Gamma

130   135   140   145   150   155   160   165   170

Futures Price

CHAPTER 10

Spreading Strategies

Spreading strategies are among the most common strategies done in option markets. In a spreading strategy a trader will take a position in one contract or set of contracts, and an opposing position in a different contract or set of contracts. The opposing positions may be directional (delta), or they may be volatility (gamma or vega) positions.

1.

CONTRACT A	CONTRACT B	CONTRACT C	CONTRACT D
46.75	70.30	81.80	59.15

a. buy 1 contract A and sell 1 contract C

$$-46.75 + 81.80 = \textbf{+35.05}$$

b. buy 1 contract B and sell 1 contract D

$$-70.30 + 59.15 = \textbf{-11.15}$$

c. buy 1 contract B and sell 2 contract A

$$-70.30 + (2 \times 46.75) = \textbf{+23.20}$$

d. buy 3 contract D and sell 2 contract C

$$-(3 \times 59.15) + (2 \times 81.80) = \textbf{-13.85}$$

e. buy 1 contract A, buy 1 contract D, and sell 1 contract C

$$-46.75 - 59.15 + 81.80 = \mathbf{-24.10}$$

f. buy 2 contract B, sell 1 contract C, and sell 1 contract D

$$-(2 \times 70.30) + 81.80 + 59.15 = \mathbf{+.35}$$

2. Spreading terminology is not uniform in every market. The answer given for the name or type is what is usually considered the most common term.

		NAME OR TYPE	INITIAL GAMMA	INITIAL THETA	INITIAL VEGA
a.	+1 January 70 call +1 January 70 put	long straddle	+	−	+
b.	+1 February 65 call −1 March 65 call	short call calendar or time spread	+	−	−
c.	+1 February 70 put −3 February 60 puts	put ratio spread	−	+	−
d.	+1 March 55 call −2 March 60 calls +1 March 65 call	long call butterfly	−	+	−
e.	+1 March 65 call +1 March 75 put	long strangle (guts)	+	−	+
f.	+1 April 105 call −1 April 115 call −1 April 120 call	long call Christmas tree or ladder	−	+	−
g.	+1 June 100 put −1 April 100 put	long put calendar or time spread	−	+	+
h.	+1 May 95 call −1 May 100 call −1 May 110 call +1 May 115 call	long call condor	−	+	−
i.	+2 April 120 calls −1 April 110 calls	call ratio spread	+	−	+

(continued on next page)

		NAME OR TYPE	INITIAL GAMMA	INITIAL THETA	INITIAL VEGA
j.	−1 June 105 put −1 June 120 call	**short strangle**	−	+	−
k.	−1 July 25 put +2 July 30 puts −1 July 35 put	**short put butterfly**	+	−	+
l.	+1 September 30 put +1 September 35 put −1 September 45 put	**short put Christmas tree or ladder**	+	−	+
m.	+1 July 35 put −1 August 35 put	**short put calendar or time spread**	+	−	−
n.	+1 July 40 put +1 July 50 call	**long strangle**	+	−	+
o.	+1 August 40 call −2 August 45 calls	**call ratio spread**	−	+	−
p.	−1 October 30 put +1 October 35 put +1 October 40 put −1 October 45 put	**short put condor**	+	−	+
q.	+3 November 1850 puts −2 November 1900 puts	**put ratio spread**	+	−	+
r.	+1 December 2000 call −1 October 2000 call	**long call calendar or time spread**	−	+	+
s.	−1 November 1900 call +2 November 2000 calls −1 November 2100 call	**short call butterfly**	+	−	+
t.	−1 December 2200 call −1 December 2200 put	**short straddle**	−	+	−

3.

	OPTION	PRICE	DELTA
a.	July 85 straddle	3.17 + 4.81 = **7.98**	46 − 54 = **−8**
b.	July/May 80 call calendar spread	5.68 − 4.19 = **1.49**	66 − 66 = **0**
c.	May 75/85 1×2 call spread	7.94 − (2 × 1.77) = **4.40**	88 − (2 × 38) = **12**
d.	July 80/85/90 put butterfly	(2.40 + 8.15) − (2 × 4.81) = **.93**	(−72 −34) − (2 × −54) = **+2**
e.	July 75/90 strangle	.96 + 1.59 = **2.55**	−17 +28 = **+11**
f.	May 80/85/90 put Christmas tree	7.97 −4.18 −1.64 = **2.15**	−83 +62 +34 = **+13**
g.	July 75/85 1×3 put spread	4.81 − (3 × .96) = **1.93**	−54 − (3 × −17) = **−3**
h.	May 75/80/85/90 call condor	(7.94 + .59) − (4.19 + 1.77) = **2.57**	+88 −66 −38 +17 = **+1**
i.	July 80/85 "guts" strangle	5.68 + 4.81 = **10.49**	66 −54 = **+12**

4.

	UNDERLYING PRICE	DIRECTIONAL OUTLOOK	IMPLIED VOLATILITY	SPREAD CHOICES
a.	90	bullish	unusually high	**long an 85 call / short a 90 call**
b.	55	bearish	unusually low	**long a 55 put / short a 50 put**
c.	127	bearish	unusually high	**long a 135 call / short a 125 call**
d.	2,485	bullish	unusually low	**long a 2,500 call / short a 2,700 call**

5. a.

	THE STOCK PRICE RISES SHARPLY	TIME PASSES WITH NO MOVEMENT	IMPLIED VOLATILITY RISES
1 March 80 call −1 March 90 call	+	−	+

b.

	THE STOCK PRICE RISES SHARPLY	TIME PASSES WITH NO MOVEMENT	IMPLIED VOLATILITY RISES
+2 March 75 puts −1 March 80 put	+	−	+

c.

	INTEREST RATES RISE SHARPLY	TIME PASSES WITH NO MOVEMENT	IMPLIED VOLATILITY FALLS
+1 March 80 put −1 June 80 put	+	−	+

d.

	THE STOCK PRICE FALLS SHARPLY	TIME PASSES WITH VOLATILITY FALLS	IMPLIED NO MOVEMENT
+1 June 75 put −2 June 80 puts +1 June 85 put	−	+	+

e.

	THE STOCK PRICE RISES SHARPLY	TIME PASSES WITH NO MOVEMENT	IMPLIED VOLATILITY RISE
+1 March 80 call +1 March 80 put	+	−	+

f.

	THE STOCK PRICE RISES SHARPLY	THE DIVIDEND IS REDUCED	IMPLIED VOLATILITY FALLS
−1 March 80 call +1 June 80 call	−	+	−

g.

	THE STOCK PRICE FALLS SHARPLY	TIME PASSES WITH NO MOVEMENT	IMPLIED VOLATILITY FALLS
−3 June 85 calls +1 June 75 call	−	+	+

h.

	INTEREST RATES FALL SHARPLY	THE DIVIDEND IS INCREASED	IMPLIED VOLATILITY FALLS
−1 March 80 put +1 June 80 put	+	+	−

6.

a. +1 April 40 call / −1 April 45 call   **highest**
    +1 April 55 call / −1 April 60 call   **lowest**

b. +1 April 40 put / −1 April 45 put   **lowest**
    +1 April 45 put / −1 April 55 put   **highest**

c. +1 April 45 call / −1 April 50 call   **highest**
    +1 April 50 call / −1 April 55 call   **lowest**

d. +1 April 60 call / +1 April 60 put   **highest**
    +1 April 50 call / +1 April 50 put   **lowest**

e. +1 April 50 call / +1 April 50 put   **lowest**
    +1 June 55 call / +1 June 55 put   **highest**

f. +1 April 40 put / −2 April 50 puts / +1 April 60 put   **highest**
    +1 April 40 call / −2 April 45 calls / +1 April 50 call   **lowest**

g. +1 April 40 call / −2 April 45 calls / +1 April 50 call   **lowest**
    +1 April 40 put / −2 April 50 puts / +1 April 60 put   **highest**

h. +1 June 50 call / −1 April 50 call   **highest**
    +1 June 40 put / −1 April 40 put   **lowest**

CHAPTER 11

Synthetic Equivalents

1.

a.	+1 January 60 call −1 January 60 put	**long an underlying contract**
b.	−1 February 1000 put −1 underlying contract	**−1 February 1000 call**
c.	+1 March 150 call +1 March 150 put	**long straddle**
d.	−1 April 600 call −1 underlying contract	**none of the above**
e.	−1 May 75 call +1 underlying contract	**−1 May 75 put**
f.	−2 June 5000 puts −1 underlying contract	**short straddle**
g.	+1 July 40 call +1 underlying contract	**none of the above**
h.	+1 August 1500 call −1 underlying contract	**+1 August 1500 put**
i.	+1 September 200 put +1 underlying	**+1 September 200 call**
j.	+1 October 80 put −1 underlying contract	**none of the above**
k.	−1 November 125 call +1 November 125 put	**short an underlying contract**
l.	+2 December 55 calls −1 underlying contract	**long straddle**

m.	+1 March 60 put −1 March 65 put −1 March 70 call +1 March 75 call	**long condor**
n.	−1 September 225 put +1 September 250 put +1 September 250 call −1 September 275 call	**short butterfly**

2. **a.** In order to show that a long iron butterfly is equivalent to a short butterfly, we can rewrite all the contracts as the same type, either all calls or all puts. Rewriting the puts as calls we have:

~~−1 October 80 put~~ −1 October 80 call / +1 underlying contract

~~+1 October 85 put~~ +1 October 85 call / −1 underlying contract

+1 October 85 call

−1 October 90 call

The underlying contracts cancel out, leaving us with:

−1 October 80 call

+2 October 85 calls

−1 October 90 call

b. In order to show that a short iron condor is equivalent to a long condor, we can rewrite all the contracts as the same type, either all calls or all puts. Rewriting the puts as calls we have:

~~+1 October 75 put~~ +1 October 75 call / −1 underlying contract

~~−1 October 80 put~~ −1 October 80 call / +1 underlying contract

−1 October 85 call

+1 October 90 call

The underlying contracts cancel out, leaving us with:

+1 October 75 call

−1 October 80 call

−1 October 85 call

+1 October 90 call

3. In order to rewrite the position in terms of only calls, we can rewrite all the puts as synthetic puts:

−16 underlying contracts

−9 May 45 calls

~~−11 May 45 puts~~   −11 May 45 calls / +11 underlying contracts

+26 May 50 calls

~~+14 May 50 puts~~   +14 May 50 calls / −14 underlying contracts

+19 May 55 calls

~~−19 May 55 puts~~   −19 May 55 calls / +19 underlying contracts

Combining contracts we have:

−20 May 45 calls / +40 May 50 calls (1 × 2 ratio spread)

4. We can rewrite all the calls as synthetic calls, or all the puts as synthetic puts. If we rewrite the calls:

    −8 underlying contracts

    ~~+21 July 70 calls~~   +21 July 70 puts / +21 underlying contracts

    −56 July 70 puts

    ~~+30 July 80 calls~~   +30 July 80 puts / +30 underlying contracts

    +40 July 80 puts

    ~~−43 July 90 calls~~   −43 July 90 puts / −43 underlying contracts

    +8 July 90 puts

Combining contracts, we have:

    −35 July 70 puts / +70 July 80 puts / −35 July 90 puts (short butterfly)

CHAPTER 12

Synthetic Pricing and Arbitrage

Basic put-call parity:

$$\text{call price} - \text{put price} = (\text{forward price} - \text{exercise price}) / (1 + \text{interest rate} \times \text{time})$$

1. Options on futures; futures-type settlement (an effective interest rate of zero)

    a. Futures price = 61.75

EXERCISE PRICE	45	50	55	60	65	70	75	80
call price	**16.80**	11.90	**7.50**	4.05	**1.85**	.70	**.25**	.10
put price	.05	**.15**	.75	**2.30**	5.10	**8.95**	13.50	**18.35**

    b.

FUTURES PRICE	EXERCISE PRICE	CALL PRICE	PUT PRICE
152.65	140	15.80	**3.15**
461.51	475	6.99	20.48
80.87	**80**	4.48	3.61
26.77	25	**1.99**	.22
3,352.00	3,500	1.45	**149.45**
760.85	**800**	4.65	43.80
1,441.20	1,500	**12.90**	71.70
54.11	55	1.56	2.45

c. What is the best way to . . .

i. buy a June futures contract?

Instead of buying the actual futures contract, you can buy the futures contract synthetically by buying the call at a price of 15.15 and selling the put at a price of 4.85:

$$15.15 - 4.85 = ? - 400$$

The price at which you can buy a futures contract synthetically is **410.30**. This is .05 *better* than buying the actual futures contract.

ii. sell the June 400 call?

Instead of selling the June 400 call, you can sell the June 400 call synthetically by selling the June 400 put at a price of 4.85 and selling the futures contract at a price of 410.15:

$$? - 4.85 = 410.15 - 400$$

The price at which you can sell the June 400 call synthetically is **15.00**. This is .10 *better* than selling the actual June 400 call.

iii. sell the June 400 put?

Instead of selling the June 400 put, you can sell the June 400 put synthetically by selling the June 400 call at a price of 14.90 and buying the futures contract at a price of 410.35:

$$14.90 - ? = 410.35 - 400$$

The price at which you can sell the June 400 put synthetically is **4.55**. This is .30 *worse* than selling the actual June 400 put.

2. Options on futures; stock-type settlement

a.

EXERCISE PRICE	1,050	1,100	1,150	1,200	1,250	1,300	1,350	1,400
call price	192.45	**146.56**	104.85	**69.67**	42.65	**23.93**	12.30	**5.74**
put price	**1.27**	4.40	**11.71**	25.55	**47.55**	77.85	**115.24**	157.70

b.

FUTURES PRICE	EXERCISE PRICE	TIME TO EXPIRATION (DAYS)	INTEREST RATE	CALL PRICE	PUT PRICE
258.77	300	23	3.72%	.20	41.33
114.47	120	74	**2.69%**	2.28	7.78
47.62	45	160	7.65%	**4.51**	1.98
2,264.75	2,200	208	1.75%	149.04	84.93
858.40	900	91	4.00%	17.80	**58.99**

c. When options on futures are subject to futures-type settlement the delta of the synthetic is $100/(1 + r \times t)$. The total delta is therefore $100/(1 + r \times t) - 100$.

interest rates are 8.00%

i. 12 months to expiration? **approximately −7.4**

ii. 9 months to expiration? **approximately −5.7**

iii. 6 months to expiration? **approximately −3.8**

iv. 3 months to expiration? **approximately −2.0**

The position has a total negative delta because you can earn interest on the variation credit if the futures contract declines.

3. Options on stock

    a.

EXERCISE PRICE	130	135	140	145	150	155	160	165
call price	**20.60**	16.30	**12.50**	9.25	**6.55**	4.45	**2.95**	1.85
put price	.70	**1.37**	2.55	**4.27**	6.55	**9.43**	12.90	**16.78**

    b.

STOCK PRICE	EXERCISE PRICE	TIME TO EXPIRATION (DAYS)	INTEREST RATE	EXPECTED DIVIDENDS	CALL PRICE	PUT PRICE
260.03	270	34	5.69%	2.00	**3.50**	14.04
23.97	25	137	3.32%	**.17**	1.31	2.20
446.75	450	96	**4.26%**	1.75	17.30	17.30
86.05	80	73	4.50%	.62	8.27	**2.12**
126.00	125	64	8.00%	.95	5.72	3.93
59.15	50	**233**	2.71%	0	10.70	.70

    c. −1 March 80 call
       +1 March 80 put
       +1 stock contract

       i. the stock price rises: **0**

       ii. the dividend is increased: **+**

       iii. implied volatility rises: **0**

       iv. the stock price falls: **0**

       v. interest rates rise: **−**

       vi. implied volatility falls: **0**

vii. the dividend is reduced: −

viii. interest rates fall: +

4. Boxes

   a.

LOWER EXERCISE PRICE	HIGHER EXERCISE PRICE	TIME TO EXPIRATION (DAYS)	INTEREST RATE	BOX VALUE
80	90	78	3.30%	**9.93**
125	150	35	5.00%	**24.88**
320	360	143	1.93%	**39.70**
40	45	283	**7.65%**	4.72
1,100	1,300	**309**	2.11%	196.49

   b.

LOWER EXERCISE PRICE	HIGHER EXERCISE PRICE	TIME TO EXPIRATION (DAYS)	INTEREST RATE	CALL SPREAD	PUT SPREAD
65	80	54	2.71%	10.22	**4.72**
20	25	122	8.60%	**2.86**	2.00
2,500	2,600	256	**4.41%**	80.50	16.50
700	775	**180**	1.91%	33.28	41.02

5. Rolls

   a.

EXERCISE PRICE	TIME TO SHORT-TERM EXPIRATION (DAYS)	TIME TO LONG-TERM EXPIRATION (DAYS)	INTEREST RATE	DIVIDENDS BETWEEN EXPIRATIONS	ROLL VALUE
70	35	63	3.01%	0	**.16**
125	15	78	7.75%	.32	**1.32**
35	44	72	2.63%	**.18**	−.11
100	65	156	5.64%	**.52**	.84

b.

EXERCISE PRICE	TIME TO SHORT-TERM EXPIRATION (DAYS)	TIME TO LONG-TERM EXPIRATION (DAYS)	INTEREST RATE	DIVIDENDS BETWEEN EXPIRATIONS	CALL CALENDAR SPREAD	PUT CALENDAR SPREAD
200	21	49	1.96%	.15	2.00	**1.85**
45	8	43	8.21%	.10	**1.50**	1.25
90	65	93	3.83%	**.56**	2.55	2.85
115	30	121	6.08%	**.65**	3.45	2.40

6. It may seem that we can't fill in the missing values without a stock price and interest rate. But we can infer an interest rate from the price of the 130 / 160 box:

$$\text{interest rate} = [(30/\text{box price}) - 1] / (73/365) = [(30/29.76 - 1]/(73/365) = \textbf{4.03\%}$$

With an interest rate (4.03%), we can use put-call parity at either the 130 or 160 exercise price to infer the stock price:

$$\text{stock price} = \text{call price} - \text{put price} + \text{exercise price} / (1+\text{rate} \times \text{time})$$

$$= 19.92 - 1.23 + 130/(1+.0403 \times 73/365) = \textbf{147.65}$$

$$\text{or} = 3.35 - 14.42 + 160/(1+.0403 \times 73/365) = \textbf{147.65}$$

With an interest rate of 4.03% and a stock price of 147.65 we can use put-call parity to fill in the price for the 120 call, the 140 put, 150 call, and the 170 put.

	120	130	140	150	160	170
calls	**28.90**	19.92	12.37	**6.84**	3.35	1.46
puts	.29	1.23	**3.60**	7.99	14.42	**22.45**

7.

$$\text{long iron butterfly} = \text{long straddle} + \text{short strangle}$$

$$\text{long iron butterfly} \approx \text{short butterfly}$$

$$\text{butterfly price} + \text{iron butterfly price} = \text{amount between exercise prices}$$

$$? + 3.25 = 10.00$$

$$\text{iron butterfly price} = 6.75$$

$$\text{strangle price} = 9.50 - 6.75 = \mathbf{2.75}$$

8.

$$\text{long condor} = \text{long call spread} + \text{short call spread}$$

$$\text{long condor} \approx \text{short iron condor}$$

$$\text{condor price} + \text{iron condor price} = \text{amount between two outside prices}$$

$$? + 2.00 = 5.00$$

$$\text{condor price} = 3.00$$

$$50 \,/\, 55 \text{ call spread} = 4.00 - 3.00 = \mathbf{1.00}$$

CHAPTER 13

Early Exercise of American Options

1. Options on futures; stock-type settlement

OPTION	FUTURES PRICE	TIME TO EXPIRATION	INTEREST RATE	LOWER ARBITRAGE BOUNDARY	
				EUROPEAN	AMERICAN
40 put	37.66	134 days	3.95%	2.31	2.34
90 call	94.50	4 months	6.00%	4.41	4.50
150 call	143.80	7 weeks	4.10%	0	0
500 put	425.00	83 days	5.25%	74.12	75.00
1200 put	1,255.00	1 month	2.37%	0	0
3000 call	3,463.00	44 weeks	1.20%	458.35	463.00

2. a. Options on stock

EXERCISE PRICE	STOCK PRICE	TIME TO EXPIRATION	INTEREST RATE	EXPECTED DIVIDEND	FORWARD PRICE	EUROPEAN		AMERICAN	
						CALL	PUT	CALL	PUT
25	24.75	30 weeks	7.60%	.0	25.84	.80	0	.80	.25
65	68.75	2 months	2.30%	.50	68.51	3.50	0	3.75	0
90	88.90	180 days	4.66%	.33	90.61	.60	0	.60	1.10
130	116.50	5 weeks	6.80%	.45	116.81	0	13.10	0	13.50
500	510.80	1 month	8.74%	5.80	508.72	8.66	0	10.80	0
550	552.15	8 weeks	5.25%	8.30	548.31	0	1.68	2.15	1.68
1,350	1,355.00	27 days	1.75%	9.25	1,347.50	0	2.49	5.00	2.49
2,500	2,231.40	102 days	3.13%	1.56	2,249.36	0	248.47	0	268.60

LOWER ARBITRAGE BOUNDARY

b. i. True

   ii. False

c. If the forward price is equal to the exercise price

d. i. Buy the stock and immediately exercise the put

   ii. total profit = intrinsic value – price = 1.10 – .85 = **.25**

e. i. Sell the stock and carry the position to expiration.

   ii. the stock price at expiration is 30? **.20**

   iii. the stock price at expiration is 20? **5.20**

   total profit = lower arbitrage boundary – option price + amount by which the option is out-of-the-money

3. a. Interest that can be earned = (1,325 – 1,200) × .06 × 26 / 365 = .53
   The price of the March 1200 put (the option's volatility value) must be less than .53.

b. Daily interest that can be earned = (1,325 – 1,200) × .06 / 365 = .0205
   The theta of the March 1200 put must be less than .0205 (in absolute value).

4. Call options on stock

a. Interest cost of exercising now = 50 × .04 × 35/365 = .19
   interest cost + volatility value = .19 + .20 = .39
   Therefore, exercise now in order to collect the dividend since .39 < .50

b. In 14 days, since exercise of a stock option call can only be optimal the day before the stock pays the dividend.

c. Interest cost the day before the stock pays the dividend = 50 × .04 × 21/365 = .12
   The put must be trading at a price less than .50 – .12 = **.38**

    d. Buy the May 50 put since long put + long stock = long call

    e. .38 – the put price

5. Put options on stock

    a. Interest that can be earned each day = $95 \times .05/365 = .013$
       blackout period = $.25 / .013 \approx$ **19 (days)**

    b. Interest that can be earned = $95 \times .05 \times 54 /365 = .70$
       interest value > volatility value + dividend
       .70 > volatility value + .25
       The July 95 call must be trading at a price **less than .45**.

    c. One day's worth of interest value must be greater than one day's worth of volatility value.
       One day's worth of interest value = .013
       One day's worth of volatility value = the theta of the July 95 call
       The theta must be **less than .013** (in absolute value).

    d. No. At a minimum, you should wait for the theta to fall below .013.

    e. 10 days is within the blackout period. You should never exercise during this period, regardless of the call price.

6. **a.** 80 call: A call can never be an early exercise until the day before the stock pays the dividend. **No, do not exercise now.**

    b. 45 put:

$$\text{Interest that can be earned each day} = 45 \times .0615/365 = .0075$$

$$\text{Blackout period} = .15 / .0075 = 20 \text{ days}$$

No, do not exercise now.

c. 100 call:

$$\text{Interest lost} = 100 \times .0233 \times 51/365 = .33$$

$$\text{Interest} + \text{volatility value} = .33 + .15 = .48 < .59$$

The early exercise criteria holds over the entire life and the next day.
Yes, exercise now.

d. 150 put:

$$\text{interest earned} = 150 \times .0749 \times 64/365 = 1.97$$

$$\text{volatility value} = .75$$

$$\text{daily interest} = 150 \times .0749 / 365 = .0308$$

$$\text{daily theta} = .0239$$

The early exercise criteria holds over the entire life and the next day.
Yes, exercise now.

e. 125 call:

$$\text{Interest lost} = 125 \times .0562 \times 39/365 = .75$$

$$\text{Interest} + \text{volatility value} = .75 + .31 = 1.06 > 1.00$$

The early exercise criteria does not hold over the entire life.
No, do not exercise now.

f. 275 put:

$$\text{interest earned} = 275 \times .0378 \times 41/365 = 1.17$$

$$\text{volatility value} = .66$$

$$\text{daily interest} = 275 \times .0378 / 365 = .0285$$

$$\text{daily theta} = .0362$$

The early exercise criteria holds over the entire life but not over the next day.
No, do not exercise now.

7. If the 50 call is exercised for the dividend, the interest cost will be $50 \times .08 \times 10/52 = .77$

   This is greater than the dividend of .75. Unless interest rates fall, the 50 call (indeed, any call with an exercise price above 50) will never be exercised early

8. **a.** If implied volatility falls

   If implied volatility falls you give up less volatility value when you exercise.

   b. i. If you are short stock

   If you are short stock your position earns a lower interest rate. You are therefore giving up less interest value when you exercise.

   ii. If you are long stock

   If you are either short stock or have no stock position, early exercise will result in a short stock position on which you earn a lower interest rate. You are more likely to exercise early when you earn a higher interest rate (the long stock rate).

9. **a.** The minimum value will occur if none of the options will ever be exercised early. In that case, the box will have the same value as a European box: $(175 - 150) / (1 + .075 \times 38 / 365) = \mathbf{24.81}$

   Neither option will be exercised early if implied volatility is very high.

   b. Both calls will be exercised in 15 days (the day before the dividend is paid), resulting in an interest credit over the remaining 23 days of $25.00 \times .075 \times 23 / 365 = .12$.

   The box should be worth $24.81 + .12 = \mathbf{24.93}$

   c. Both puts will be exercised in 16 days (the day the dividend is paid), resulting in an interest credit over the remaining 22 days of $25.00 \times .075 \times 22 /365 = .11$.

   The box should be worth $24.81 + .11 = \mathbf{24.92}$.

d. There will be an interest loss of $150 \times .075 \times 23/365 = .71$.

There will be a credit equal to the amount of the dividend, 1.15.

The box should be worth $24.81 - .71 + 1.15 = \textbf{25.25}$.

e. The June 175 put will be exercised in 16 days (the day the dividend is paid), resulting in an interest credit over the remaining 22 days of $175 \times .075 \times 22/365 = .79$.

The box should be worth $24.81 + .79 = \textbf{25.60}$.

f. When the June 150 call is exercised there will be an interest loss of $150 \times .075 \times 23/365 = .71$, but a credit equal to the amount of the dividend of 1.15.

When the June 175 put is exercised there will be an interest credit of $175 \times .075 \times 22/365 = .79$.

The box should be worth $24.81 - .71 + 1.15 + .79 = \textbf{26.04}$.

Both the June 150 call and the June 175 put are likely to be exercised early if in 15 days both options are in-the-money (the stock is between 150 and 175, ideally close to 162.50) and implied volatility is very low.

CHAPTER 14

The Black-Scholes Model

1. **a.** **i.** $S/X = .954667$

      ii. $\ln(S/X) = -.046393$

      iii. t (in years) $= 86 / 365 = .235616$

      iv. $\sqrt{t} = .485403$

      v. $\sigma\sqrt{t} = .142223$

      vi. $rt = .012841$

      vii. $e^{-rt} = .987241$

      viii. $d_1 = -.164799$

      ix. $d_2 = -.307022$

      x. $N(d_1) = .434551$

      xi. $N(d_2) = .379413$

      xii. call value $= 3.020946$

      xiii. call delta $= .435$ (43.5)

    b. Traders sometimes use the delta, $N(d_1)$, as an approximation of the probability that an option will finish in-the-money. The true probability that an option will finish in-the-money is $N(d_2)$.

    $$N(d_2) = .3794 \ (37.94\%)$$

2. a.   **i.** $F/X = 1.00$

    ii. $\ln(F/X) = 0$

    iii. t (in years) = 149 / 365 = **.408219**

    iv. $\sqrt{t} = $ **.638920**

    v. $\sigma\sqrt{t} = $ **.120436**

    vi. $rt = $ **.014696**

    vii. $e^{-rt} = $ **.985412**

    viii. $d_1 = $ **.060218**

    ix. $d_2 = $ **−.060218**

    x. $N(d_1) = $ **.524009**

    xi. $N(d_2) = $ **.475991**

    xii. $N(-d_1) = $ **.475991**

    xiii. $N(-d_2) = $ **.524009**

    xiv. $n(d_1) = $ **.398220**

    xv. put value = **56.7810**

    xvi. put delta $[N(d_1) - 1] = $ **−.4760 (−47.60)**

    xvii. put gamma = **.002715 (0.2715)**

    xviii. put theta = −67.419302 / 365 = **−.184710**

    xix. put vega = 300.8626 / 100 = **3.008626**

    xx. put rho = −23.1791 / 100 = **−.231791**

b.
$$\text{One standard deviation} = 1200.00 \times .120436 = 144.52$$

$$\text{Expected value of the 1200 call} \approx 40\% \times \text{one standard deviation} = .40 \times 144.52 = 57.81$$

$$\text{Estimated theoretical value} = \text{present value of } 57.81 = 57.81 \times .9854 = \mathbf{56.97} \text{ (compared to 56.78)}$$

| CHAPTER 15 |

Binomial Pricing

1. **a.** $p = [(1 + .06 \times 2/12) - .90] / (1.15 - .90) = \mathbf{.44}$

$1 - p = 1 - .44 = \mathbf{.56}$

b. $Su = 1.15 \times 82.50 = \mathbf{94.875}$

$Sd = .90 \times 82.50 = \mathbf{74.25}$

c. 80 call: at Su $94.875 - 80 = \mathbf{14.875}$, at Sd $74.25 = \mathbf{0}$

80 put: at $Sd = \mathbf{0}$, at $Su = 80 - 74.25 = \mathbf{5.75}$

d. 80 call: $(.44 \times 14.875 + 0) / (1+.06 \times 2/12) = \mathbf{6.48}$

80 put: $(0 + .56 \times 5.75) / (1+.06 \times 2/12) = \mathbf{3.19}$

e. $C - P = (F - X) / (1 + r \times t)$

$F = 82.50 \times (1+.06 \times 2/12) = 83.325$

$(F - X) / (1 + r \times t) = (83.325 - 80) / (1 + .06 \times 2/12) = 3.325 / 1.01 = 3.29$

$C - P = 6.48 - 3.19 = 3.29$

f. $\Delta_c = (C_u - C_d) / (Su - Sd) = (14.875 - 0) / (94.875 - 74.25) = \mathbf{.721 \ (72.1)}$

$\Delta_p = (P_u - P_d) / (Su - Sd) = (0 - 5.75) / (94.875 - 74.25) = \mathbf{-.279 \ (-27.9)}$

g. buy one 80 call at a price of 6.48

sell .721 shares of stock at a price of 82.50

total cash flow = −6.48 + (.721 × 82.50) = +53.00 (credit of 53.00)

interest earned on the cash flow = 53.00 × .06 × 2/12 = .53

If stock moves up to 94.875

(14.875 − 6.48) − .721 × (94.875 − 82.50) = −.53

−.53 +.53 = 0

If stock moves down to 74.25

−6.48 + .721 × (82.50 − 74.25) = −.53

−.53 +.53 = 0

h. buy one 80 put at a price of 3.19 − .25 = 2.94

buy .279 shares of stock at a price of 82.50

total cash flow = −2.94 − (.279 × 82.50) = −25.96 (debit of 25.96)

interest lost on the cash flow = −25.96 × .06 × 2/12 = −.26

If stock moves up to 94.875

−2.94 + .279 × (94.875 − 82.50) = +.51

+.51 − .26 = +.25

If stock moves down to 74.25

$(5.75 - 2.94) - .279 \times (82.50 - 74.25) = +.51$

$+.51 - .26 = +.25$

i. $Su = 1.15 \times 82.50 - 1.50 = 93.375$

$Sd = .90 \times 82.50 - 1.50 = 72.75$

European 70 call: $(.44 \times 23.375 + .56 \times 2.75) / (1 + .06 \times 2/12) = 11.71$

American 70 call: maximum of (European value, intrinsic value) = maximum $(11.71, 82.50 - 70) = 12.50$

You should exercise the 70 call now in order not to lose the dividend.

j. $p = [(1 + 1.00 \times 2/12) - .90] / (1.15 - .90) = 1.067$

$1 - p = 1 - 1.067 = -.067$

No one would ever buy the stock. You would always be better leaving your money in the bank and earning a high rate of interest.

p and $1 - p$ are sometimes referred to as pseudo-probabilities since they can fall outside the normal range for a probability of 0 to 1.00.

2. a. $1 + .04 \times 10/52 = \mathbf{1.0077}$

  b. $u = e^{.27 \times \sqrt{10/52}} = \mathbf{1.1257}$

   $d = e^{-.27 \times \sqrt{10/52}} = \mathbf{.8883}$

   $p = [(1 + .04 \times 10/52) - .8883] / (1.1257 - .8883) = \mathbf{.5029}$

   $1 - p = 1 - .5029 = \mathbf{.4971}$

c. $1,278.00 \times \text{uuu} = \textbf{1,823.04}$ $(S_{3,3})$

$1,278.00 \times \text{uud} = \textbf{1,438.64}$ $(S_{3,2})$

$1,278.00 \times \text{udd} = \textbf{1,135.30}$ $(S_{3,1})$

$1,278.00 \times \text{ddd} = \textbf{895.91}$ $(S_{3,0})$

d. $1,823.04$: $.5029^3 = \textbf{.1272}$

$1,438.64$: $.5029^2 \times .4971 = \textbf{.1257}$

$1,135.30$: $.5029 \times .4971^2 = \textbf{.1243}$

895.91: $.4971^3 = \textbf{.1228}$

e. Number of paths to $S_{3,3}$: **1** (uuu)

Number of paths to $S_{3,2}$: **3** (udu, uud, duu)

Number of paths to $S_{3,1}$: **3** (udd, dud, ddu)

Number of paths to $S_{3,0}$: **1** (ddd)

f. $1,823.04$: **0**

$1,438.64$: **0**

$1,135.30$: $1,300 - 1,135.30 = \textbf{164.70}$

895.91: $1,300 - 895.91 = \textbf{404.09}$

g. $[(164.70 \times .1243 \times 3) + (404.09 \times .1228)] / 1.0077^3 = (61.42 + 49.62) / 1.0233 = \textbf{108.51}$

h.

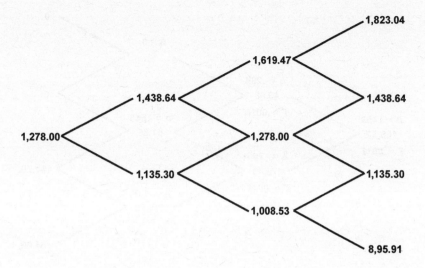

i.

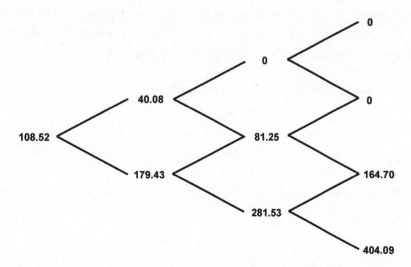

j.

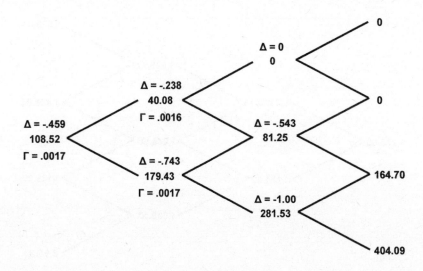

k. The theta is the change in option value if the underling price remains unchanged. The last point on the binomial tree at which the price is unchanged is at $S_{2,1}$. This is a period of 20 weeks. The approximate weekly theta is therefore $(81.25 - 108.52) / 20 = \mathbf{-1.364}$.

3. a.

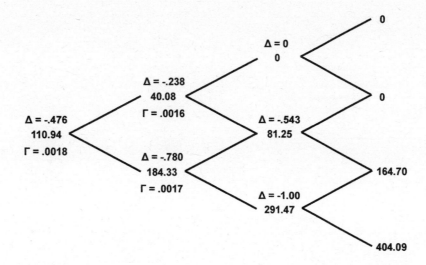

Note the change in value of $C_{2,0}$ from 281.53 (the European value) to 291.47 (intrinsic value).

b. $(81.25 - 110.94) / 20 = \mathbf{-1.485}$

CHAPTER 16

Hedging Strategies

1. **a.** sell a futures contract

   sell a call

   buy a put

   b. sell a futures contract: **v, vi**

   sell a call: **i, iv, vii**

   buy a put: **ii, iii, viii**

   c. i. **sell a call**. When implied volatility is high, you should prefer to sell options.

   ii. **buy a put**. When implied volatility is low, you should prefer to buy options.

2. You are currently long stock, with the stock trading at a price close to 50.

   a. buy a 40 call calendar spread

   buy a 40 put calendar spread

   sell a 60 call calendar spread

   sell a 60 put calendar spread

   buy a 60 straddle

   sell a 40 straddle

   sell a 45 / 50 call spread

buy a 45 / 50 put spread

sell a 50 / 55 call spread

buy a 50 / 55 put spread

b. buy a 40 call calendar spread: **iii, iv, vi**

buy a 40 put calendar spread: **iii, iv, vi**

sell a 60 call calendar spread: **iii, iv, v**

sell a 60 put calendar spread: **iii, iv, v**

buy a 60 straddle: **ii, iii, vi**

sell a 40 straddle: **i, iv, v**

sell a 45 / 50 call spread: **iii, iv, v**

buy a 45 / 50 put spread: **iii, iv, vi**

sell a 50 / 55 call spread: **iii, iv, v**

buy a 50 / 55 put spread: **iii, iv, vi**

c. sell a 40 straddle

sell a 50 / 55 call spread

buy a 50 / 55 put spread

When implied volatility is high, you should prefer to create a position with a negative vega.

3. a. long a 170 call / short a 150 put

long a 150 call / short a 170 put

long a 165 call / short a 145 put

long a 145 call / short a 165 put

long a 175 call / short a 155 put

long a 155 call / short a 175 put

A short collar, used to hedge a short underlying position, always consists of a long call and short put.

b. long a 165 call / short a 145 put

long a 155 call / short a 175 put

When implied volatility is low, you should prefer to buy an option that is closer to at-the-money, and sell an option that is further away from at-the-money.

c. long a 165 call / short a 145 put

Options that are at-the-money, or slightly out-of-the-money, are usually the most liquid and therefore easiest to trade.

4. a. Buy a futures contract

Buy either a July 525 call or a July 550 call

Sell either a July 450 put or a July 475 put

b.

STRATEGY	TOTAL COST
Buy a futures contract	496.50
Buy a July 525 call at a price of 10.25 If the commodity price < 525 If the commodity price > 525	 commodity price + 10.25 525 + 10.25 = 535.25
Buy a July 550 call at a price of 5.00 If the commodity price < 550 If the commodity price > 550	 commodity price + 5.00 550 + 5.00 = 555.00
Sell a July 450 put at a price of 4.75 If the commodity price < 450 If the commodity price > 450	 450 − 4.75 = 445.25 commodity price − 4.75
Sell a July 475 put at a price of 11.50 If the commodity price < 475 If the commodity price > 475	 475 − 11.50 = 463.50 commodity price − 11.50

c.

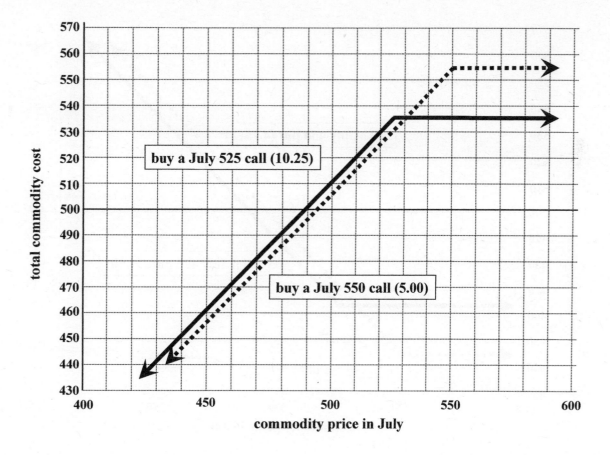

buy a July 525 call (10.25)

buy a July 550 call (5.00)

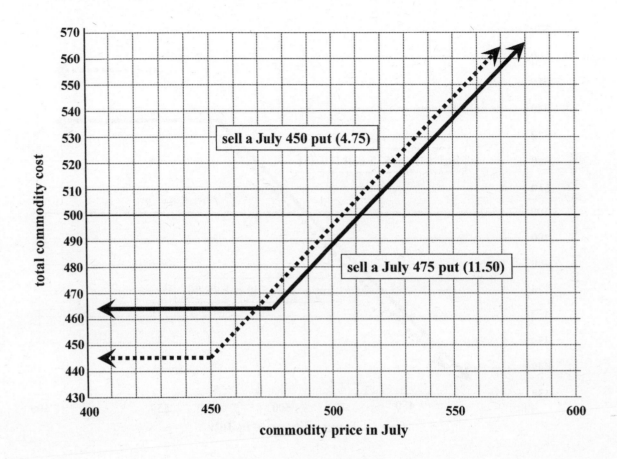

d.

If the commodity price < 475	475 + 10.25 − 11.50 = 473.75
If the commodity price > 475 and < 525	commodity price + 10.25 − 11.50 = commodity price − 1.25
If the commodity price > 525	525 + 10.25 − 11.50 = 523.75

e.

If the commodity price < 450	$450 + 5.00 - 4.75 = 450.25$
If the commodity price > 450 and < 550	commodity price $+ 5.00 - 4.75 =$ commodity price $+ .25$
If the commodity price > 550	$550 + 5.00 - 4.75 = 550.25$

f.

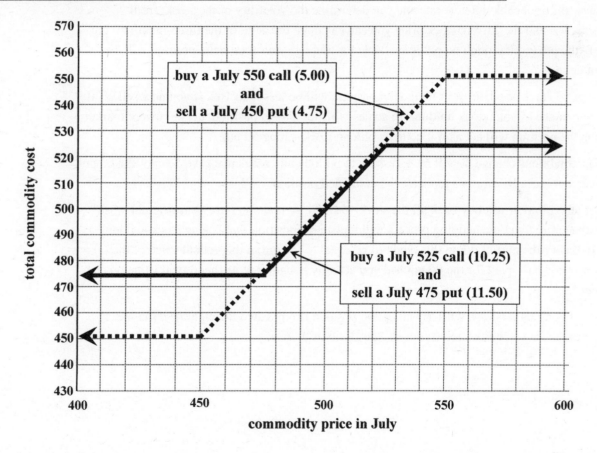

5. One possibility is to find an option dealer in the over-the-counter market who will sell you the desired put. Failing this, in theory you can replicate a position that is equivalent to long stock and long a 60 put through the dynamic hedging process. (This is also equivalent to now owning a 60 call.)

   If you know the applicable interest rate and can determine the volatility of the stock, from this information and the current stock price you can calculate the delta of the three-month 60 put. If you buy the put (even though no put is available for trading) your total delta position will be 100 + put delta.

   Since the put delta is negative, your total delta position will be less than 100. If you now sell off the correct percentage of your stock holdings to achieve this total delta position, under current market conditions the position will act as if it consists of long stock + long 60 put.

   As market conditions change, it will be necessary to periodically recalculate the delta of the 60 put and adjust your stock holdings to replicate the combined position.

   Finally, if at expiration you buy back all the stock you sold, so that you have your original stock holding, the entire dynamic hedging process will replicate a position that is long stock and long a 60 put. In theory the cost of doing this ought to be equal to the initial theoretical value of the 60 put (what you would have paid for the 60 put had you actually bought it at its theoretical value on an exchange).

   This type of hedging strategy, whereby an option position is replicated through the dynamic hedging process, is sometimes referred to as "portfolio insurance."

CHAPTER 17

Models and the Real World

1. **a. F.** The prices of the underlying contract at expiration are normally distributed.

   b. T. The prices of the underlying contract at expiration are lognormally distributed.

   c. T. The percent changes in the price of the underlying contract are normally distributed.

   d. F. The percent changes in the price of the underlying contract are lognormally distributed.

   The percent price changes are assumed to be normally distributed and continuously compounded, resulting in a lognormal distribution of prices at expiration.

   e. F. The mean of the underlying price distribution at expiration is always equal to the current price of the underlying contract.

   The mean is assumed to be equal to the forward price.

   f. T. The volatility of the underlying contract is constant over the life of the option.

   g. T. Interest rates are constant over the life of the option.

   h. F. Over the life of an option the volatility of the underlying contract may change, depending on which direction the market is moving.

   Volatility is assumed to be independent of the direction in which the underlying price is moving. Whether the market rises or falls the volatility is assumed to be constant.

   i. F. There is an optimal time to exercise an option early.

   The Black-Scholes model is a European pricing model. It does not address the question of early exercise.

j. **T.** The underlying contract can be bought or sold, without restriction, at any time over the life of the option.

k. **F.** The price of an underlying contract follows a jump-diffusion process, with occasional gaps in the prices.

The underlying price is assumed to follow a diffusion process, with no gaps in prices.

l. **F.** If held to expiration, the theoretical value of an option is determined by its implied volatility.
    In theory, the value of an option depends only on the volatility of the underlying contract because the value can be captured through a dynamic hedging process.

2. a. For exchange-traded contracts, small price changes (less than one standard deviation) tend to occur in the real world **more often than** in a true normal distribution.

   b. For exchange-traded contracts, intermediate price changes (between one and three standard deviations) tend to occur in the real world **less often than** in a true normal distribution.

   c. For exchange-traded contracts, large price changes (more than three standard deviations) tend to occur in the real world **more often than** in a true normal distribution.

   In the great majority of markets, price changes typically differ from a true normal distribution. There tend to be more small price changes, more big price changes (sometimes referred to as "fat tails"), and fewer intermediate price changes than is predicted by a true normal distribution.

   d. The value generated for a far out-of-the-money option will tend to be **higher than** the actual value of the option in the real world.

   Because the model does not know about the "fat tails" in the real world, it tends to undervalue far out-of-the-money options.

3. a. Under the assumptions of a Black-Scholes model, the trader's delta position is **approximately neutral**.

  b. If the futures market tends to become more volatile as prices rise, the trader's delta position is **positive**. The trader wants the futures price to rise because the position will profit from higher volatility.

  c. If the futures market tends to become more volatile as prices fall, the trader's delta position is **negative**. The trader wants the futures price to fall because the position will profit from higher volatility.

4. a. A gap in the price of the underlying market will have the greatest effect on the value of an **at-the-money option**.

  b. A gap in the price of the underlying market will have a greater effect on the value of a **long-term in-the-money option**.

  c. A gap in the price of the underlying market will have a greater effect on the value of a **short-term at-the-money option**. A gap will have its greatest effect on the option with the highest gamma.

  d. A price gap in the underlying market will work to the benefit of **a long option position**. A gap will work in favor of a positive gamma position.

  e. In most option markets implied volatility derived from a traditional theoretical pricing model tends to be **higher than** the volatility of the underlying contract. Option prices tend to be higher than values generated using the volatility of the underlying contract. There can be a variety of reasons for this, but one important reason is that a traditional model does not know about the price gaps that can occur in the underlying contract, and these price gaps tend to work to the benefit of option buyers. The values of options in the real world therefore tend to be greater than the values generated by the pricing model. Consequently, traders are often willing to pay a price greater than model-generated values, resulting in higher implied volatility.

5. a. **Vary the volatility used to evaluate different options, even if all options expire at the same time and have the same underlying contract.** Due to weaknesses in the model, in order to generate values that more closely approximate those in the real world, most traders vary the volatility used to evaluate options at different exercise prices.

    b. **1. D; 2. A; 3. B.** There are no markets where all exercise prices carry the same implied volatility. Even in a balanced skew, implied volatilities vary across exercise prices.

CHAPTER 18

Skewness and Kurtosis

1. **a.** The volatility is increased:

CALL WITH DELTA OF +50	PUT WITH DELTA OF –25	CALL WITH DELTA OF +5
+ + +	+ +	+

b. The skewness is reduced (becomes less positive or more negative):

PUT WITH DELTA OF –50	PUT WITH DELTA OF –25	CALL WITH DELTA OF +25
0	+	–

c. The skewness is increased (becomes more positive or less negative):

PUT WITH DELTA OF –25	PUT WITH DELTA OF –5	CALL WITH DELTA OF +5
– –	–	+

d. The kurtosis is increased (becomes more positive):

PUT WITH DELTA OF –5	CALL WITH DELTA OF +25	PUT WITH DELTA OF –50
+ +	+	0

e. The kurtosis is reduced (becomes less positive):

PUT WITH DELTA OF –5	PUT WITH DELTA OF –25	CALL WITH A DELTA OF +50
– –	–	0

f. Time passes:

PUT WITH DELTA OF –50	CALL WITH DELTA OF +25	PUT WITH DELTA OF –5
– – –	– –	–

2. a.

–5	–25	–50 / 50	+25	+5
higher	higher	equal to	lower	lower

increase skewness (make it less negative)

b.

–5	–25	–50 / 50	+25	+5
higher	higher	higher	higher	higher

reduce volatility

c.

–5	–25	–50 / 50	+25	+5
lower	lower	equal to	lower	lower

increase kurtosis

d.

–5	–25	–50 / 50	+25	+5
equal to	equal to	lower	equal to	equal to

increase volatility / reduce kurtosis

e.

−5	−25	−50 / 50	+25	+5
equal to	equal to	higher	much higher	much higher

reduce volatility / reduce skewness (make it less positive)

3. a. i. If you are short skew, you must be short options at lower exercise prices and long options at higher exercise prices:

long out-of-the-money puts / short out-of-the-money calls / long stock

short in-the-money puts / long in-the-money calls / short stock

ii. If the position consists primarily of out-of-the-money calls and puts, it must be:

long puts at lower exercise prices / short calls at higher exercise prices / long stock

b. If the price of the underlying stock begins to rise, your *gamma* position will **get shorter**. The stock is moving toward your short exercise prices.

c. If the price of the underlying stock begins to fall, your *vega* position will **get longer**. The stock is moving toward your long exercise prices.

d. If two weeks pass with no change in the stock price, your *delta* position will **get longer**. Since the options are out-of-the-money, the option deltas are moving toward zero.

e. If implied volatility rises, your *delta* position will **get shorter**. The deltas are moving toward 50 or −50.

f. i. the market moves very quickly: **falling stock price, rising implied volatility, falling interest rates, rising dividends**

ii. the market moves very slowly: **rising stock price, falling implied volatility, falling interest rates, rising dividends.**

In both cases you are long stock, so you want falling interest rates (you had to borrow the money to buy the stock) and rising dividends.

CHAPTER 19

Stock Indexes

1. a. i. price-weighted?

>index value = 25.30 + 81.70 + 46.55 = **153.55**

X	25.30 / 153.55 = **16.48%**
Y	81.70 / 153.55 = **53.21%**
Z	46.55 / 153.55 = **30.32%**

ii. capitalization-weighted?

index value = (25.30 × 9,000) + (81.70 × 5,000) + (46.55 × 3,000) =

227,700 + 408,500 + 139,650 = **775,850**

X	227,700 / 775,850 = **29.35%**
Y	408,500 / 775,850 = **52.65%**
Z	139,650 / 775,850 = **18.00%**

iii. equal-weighted?

$$\text{index value} = (25.30/25.30) + (81.70/81.70) + (46.55/46.55) = \mathbf{3.00}$$

In an equal-weighted index all stocks initially have the same weighting:

X	1 / 3 = **33.33%**
Y	1 / 3 = **33.33%**
Z	1 / 3 = **33.33%**

b. Index divisor

   i. price-weighted? 153.55 / 250 = **.6142**

   ii. capitalization-weighted? 775,850 / 250 = **3,103.40**

   iii. equal-weighted? 3 / 250 = **.012**

c. Index price = 250; stock Y splits 2 for 1. Divisor?

   i. price-weighted? (25.30 + 40.85 + 46.55) / 250 = **.4508**

   ii. capitalization-weighted? **1,642.010582** (no change)

There is no change since the capitalization of stock Y is unchanged:

$$81.70 \times 5,000 = 40.85 \times 10,000 = 408,500$$

   iii. equal-weighted? **.012** (no change)

There is no change since 81.70 / 81.70 = 34.85 / 34.85 = 1.00

d. Index price = 250; stock Z is replaced with stock W, with a price of 34.85 and 6,000 shares. Divisor?

   i. price-weighted?

$$(25.30 + 40.85 + 34.85) / 250 = \mathbf{.404}$$

ii. capitalization-weighted?

$$34.85 \times 6{,}000 = 209{,}100$$

$$(227{,}700 + 408{,}500 + 209{,}100) / 250 = \mathbf{3{,}381.2}$$

iii. equal-weighted? **.012** (no change)

There is no change since $46.55 / 46.55 = 40.85 / 40.85 = 1.00$.

e. i. Current value of the equal-weighted index?

$$[(26.54/ 25.30) + (80.25 / 81.70) + (48.93 / 46.55)] / .012 = [1.0490 + .9823 + 1.0511] / .012 = \mathbf{256.87}$$

ii. The index is now rebalanced. Divisor?

$$3.00 / 256.87 = \mathbf{.01168}$$

2. a. percent change in A $= 4.00 / 186.50 = 2.1448\%$

$$.021448 \times .0864 = .001853$$

$$(1 + .001853) \times 12{,}599.83 = \mathbf{12{,}623.18}$$

b. The rise in the price of stock A from 186.50 to 190.50 will cause its weighting in the index to change. But we can use the original price of 186.50 and weighting of 8.64%, as well as the original index price of 12,599.83, to calculate the new index price.

$$\text{percent change in A} = -8.00 / 186.50 = -4.2895\%$$

$$-.042895 \times .0864 = -.003706$$

$$\text{percent change in B} = 2.75 / 98.75 = 2.7848\%$$

$$.027848 \times .0512 = .001426$$

$$(1 - .003706 + .001426) \times 12{,}599.83 = \mathbf{12{,}571.10}$$

c. When stock A fell from 190.50 to 178.50, and stock B rose from 98.75 to 101.50, the index fell from 12,623.18 to 12,571.10. We know that .001426 of that was the result of the price change in B. Therefore:

$$(1 + ? + .001426) \times 12{,}623.18 = 12{,}571.10$$

$$(1 + ? + .001426) = 12{,}571.10 / 12{,}623.18 = .995874$$

$$? = .995874 - .001426 - 1 = -.005552$$

If stock A falls from 190.50 to 178.50, then:

$$\text{percent change in A} = -12.00 / 190.50 = -6.2992\%$$

Therefore:

$$\text{weighting of stock A} \times -.062992 = -.005552$$

$$\text{weighting of stock A} = .005552 / .062992 = \mathbf{.0881 \ (8.81\%)}$$

3. a.

L	$1{,}000{,}000 \times .2529 / 30.25 = $ **8360 shares**
M	$1{,}000{,}000 \times .4263 / 70.81 = $ **6020 shares**
N	$1{,}000{,}000 \times .3208 / 55.46 = $ **5784 shares**

b. If the index price rises, causing the futures price to rise, there will be a variation debit, resulting in an interest loss. To offset this loss, the replicating portfolio must be increased by the interest rate component.

L	$8360 \times (1 + .06 \times 3/12) = $ **8486 shares**
M	$6020 \times (1 + .06 \times 3/12) = $ **6110 shares**
N	$5784 \times (1 + .06 \times 3/12) = $ **5871 shares**

c.

L	$8360 \times (1 + .054 \times 1/12) =$ **8398 shares**
M	$6020 \times (1 + .054 \times 1/12) =$ **6047 shares**
N	$5784 \times (1 + .054 \times 1/12) =$ **5810 shares**

4. a. $(2{,}520.37 + 9.94) / [1 + (.0533 \times 72 / 365)] =$ **2,503.98**

   b. $\{[(2{,}520.37 + 9.94) / 2{,}509.80] - 1\} / (72/365) =$ **.0414 (4.14%)**

   c. $2{,}507.94 \times (1 + .0383 \times 72/365) - 2{,}520.37 =$ **6.52**

Risk Analysis

1. a. Using synthetics, we can rewrite the position as all calls (or all puts):

+12 October 45 calls

~~–87 October 45 puts~~   –87 October 45 calls / + 87 underlying

–46 October 50 calls

~~+46 October 50 puts~~   +46 October 50 calls / –46 underlying

+59 October 55 calls

~~+16 October 55 puts~~   +16 October 55 calls / –16 underlying

–25 underlying contracts

Combining contracts, we can see that the position is bear spread:

–75 October 45 calls

+75 October 55 calls

At a price close to 45, the 45 exercise price is at-the-money.

delta is **negative**

gamma is **negative**

theta is **positive**

vega is **negative**

b. At a price close to 55 the 55 exercise price is at-the-money.

>   delta is **negative**
>
>   gamma is **positive**
>
>   theta is **negative**
>
>   vega is **positive**

2. a. i. delta: $(68 \times -36.3) + (37 \times 28.1) + 1{,}200 = $ **−228.7**

    ii. gamma: $(68 \times 2.41) + (37 \times 2.17) = $ **+244.17**

    iii. theta: $(68 \times -.0189) + (37 \times -.0252) = $ **−2.2176**

    iv. vega: $(68 \times .264) + (37 \times .240) = $ **+26.832**

    v. rho: $(68 \times -.162) + (37 \times .105) = $ **−7.131**

b. 3 for 1 stock split. New stock price?

> $122.82 / 3 = $ **40.94**

c. New option and stock position?

>   **+204 November 40 puts** $(120/3 = 40; 68 \times 3 = 204)$
>
>   **+111 November 45 calls** $(135/3 = 45; 37 \times 3 = 111)$
>
>   **+3600 shares of stock** $(1200 \times 3 = 3600)$

d. stock split is 3 for 1.

	DELTA	GAMMA	THETA	VEGA	RHO
	OLD DELTA × 3	OLD GAMMA / 3	OLD THETA / 3	OLD VEGA / 3	OLD RHO
November 40 put	−36.3	7.23	−.0063	.088	−.054
November 45 call	28.1	6.51	−.0084	.080	+.035

e.   **i.**   delta: $(204 \times -36.3) + (111 \times 28.1) + 3600 = \mathbf{-686.1}$

ii.   gamma: $(204 \times 7.23) + (111 \times 6.51) = \mathbf{+2197.53}$

iii.   new theta: $(204 \times -.0063) + (111 \times -.0084) = \mathbf{-2.2176}$

iv.   new vega: $(204 \times .088) + (111 \times .080) = \mathbf{+26.832}$

v.   new rho: $(204 \times -.054) + (111 \times .035) = \mathbf{-7.131}$

f.   **i.**   new delta position: old delta position $\times$ ("y" / "x")

ii.   new gamma position: old gamma position $\times$ ("y" / "x")^2

iii.   new theta position: same as old theta position

iv.   new vega position: same as old vega position

v.   new rho position: same as old rho position

g.   new option price = old option price / ("y" / "x")

November 40 put: $4.14 / 3 = \mathbf{1.38}$

November 45 call: $2.55 / 3 = \mathbf{.85}$

3.

TIME TO EXPIRATION	1 MONTH	3 MONTHS	6 MONTHS	12 MONTHS
implied volatility	33%	30%	28%	27%

a. Mean volatility? **26%**

b.

	1-MONTH	3-MONTH	6-MONTH	12-MONTH
iii.	**30%**	**28%**	**27%**	**26%**

c.

	1-MONTH	3-MONTH	6-MONTH	12-MONTH
i.	**37%**	**33%**	**30%**	**28%**

3. a. i. total vega = –23.10 + 13.10 – 14.20 + 28.40 = **+4.20**

   ii. A positive vega position wants implied volatility to rise.

b. i. Total vega in terms of changes in March implied volatility?

EXPIRATION MONTH	VEGA	ADJUSTMENT	TOTAL ADJUSTED VEGA
March	–23.10	1.00	–23.10
April	+13.10	.80	+10.48
June	–14.20	.70	–9.94
September	+28.40	.65	+18.46
Totals	+4.20		–4.10

ii. A negative vega position wants implied volatility to fall.

iii. You would expect the position to lose approximately $3 \times -4.10 = -12.30$.

Note that the term structure of volatility turned a raw positive vega position into a negative adjusted vega position.

4. a. While several expirations might appear to be mispriced, the most noticeable seem to be the 39-week expiration (too cheap) and the 52-week expiration (too expensive).

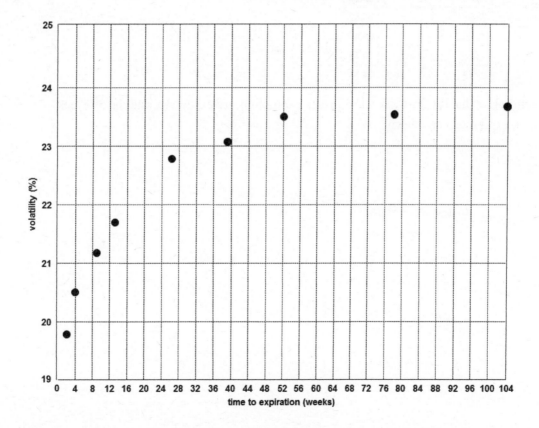

b. $\sigma_f = \sqrt{\{[(\sigma_2^2 \times t_2) - (\sigma_1^2 \times t_1)] / (t_2 - t_1)\}}$

TIME TO EXPIRATION (WEEKS)	IMPLIED VOLATILITY (%) (AT-THE-MONEY OPTIONS)	FORWARD VOLATILITY
2	19.80	
4	20.51	**21.20**
9	21.20	**21.74**
13	21.70	**22.78**
26	22.80	**23.85**
39	23.06	**23.57**
52	23.46	**24.62**
78	23.55	**23.73**
104	23.70	**24.14**

Now it seems clear that the 26-week and 52-week expirations are expensive, and the 39-week and 78-week expirations are cheap.

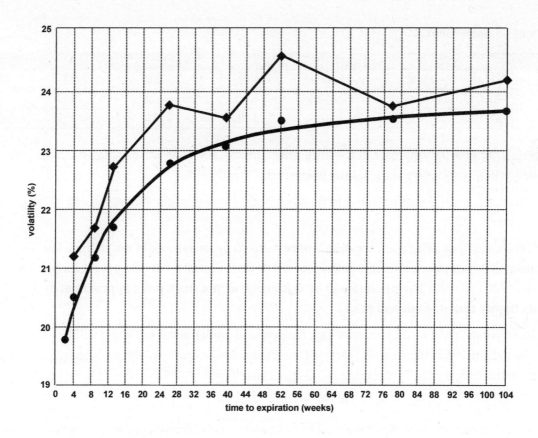

5. Stock position: –8 stock contracts

OPTIONS	TOTAL CALLS	TOTAL PUTS	TOTAL DELTA	TOTAL GAMMA	TOTAL THETA	TOTAL VEGA	TOTAL RHO
Month 1	+53	+16	+4610	+25	–2.57	+4.5	+14.4
Month 2	–80	+64	–3484	–41	+3.30	–20.2	–25.7
totals	–27	+80	+326	–16	+.73	–15.7	–11.3

a. i. best scenario: slow upward move in the stock price (positive delta / negative gamma), falling implied volatility (negative vega), falling interest rates (negative rho)

ii. worst scenario: swift downward move in the stock price, rising implied volatility, rising interest rates

b. For each point the stock price rises, the delta will be reduced by the amount of the gamma. We can estimate the stock price at which the position will be delta neutral by dividing the delta by the gamma: 326 / 16 ≈ 20. **The position will be delta neutral at a stock price approximately 20 points higher than the current price.**

c. For each percentage point increase in volatility, the potential profit (theoretical edge) will be reduced by the amount of the vega. We can estimate the implied volatility of the position by dividing the theoretical edge by the vega:

$$78 / 15.7 \approx 5$$

The implied (breakeven) volatility of the position is approximately 5 percentage points higher than the evaluation volatility of 22%, or **27%**.

d. Average delta if the stock moves up 10 points: $326 + (10 \times -16) / 2 = +246$

New theoretical edge: $78 + (2.46 \times 10) = \textbf{+102.60}$

Average delta if the stock moves down 10 points: $326 - (10 \times -16) / 2 = +406$

New theoretical edge: $78 + (4.06 \times -10) = \textbf{+37.40}$

e. **i.** On a large downward move calls will be irrelevant, while the puts will begin to act like short underlying contracts. Since the position is short 8 stock contracts and net long 80 puts, the position will act as if it is short 88 stock contracts (the downside contract position).

   ii. On a large upward move puts will be irrelevant, while the calls will begin to act like long underlying contracts. Since the position is short 8 stock contracts and net short 27 calls, the position will act as if it is short 35 stock contracts (the upside contract position).

f. In question 5a we concluded that the worst outcome includes a swift downward move in the stock price. But from question 5e.i we can see that if the downward move is really large, eventually the move will begin to work in favor of the position.

g. As volatility increases all delta values move toward 50 for calls and toward –50 for puts.

In total the position is short 27 calls, which in the extreme will act like –1,350 deltas.

In total the position is long 80 puts, which in the extreme will act like –4,000 deltas.

Together with the –800 deltas for the 8 underlying contracts, we can see that in the extreme the total position delta will move toward

$$-1350 - 4000 - 800 = \mathbf{-6150}$$

As volatility increases the position will become increasingly bearish.

h. **i.** If Month 2 volatility changes by only 75% of Month 1 volatility, the total adjusted vega is:

$$4.5 - .75 \times 20.2 \approx \mathbf{-10.65}$$

ii. With an adjusted vega of –10.65, for each percentage point increase in Month 1 volatility, the potential profit will be reduced by the amount of the adjusted vega. We can estimate the Month 1 implied volatility of the position by dividing the theoretical edge by the adjusted vega:

$$78 / 10.65 \approx 7.3$$

The implied (breakeven) volatility of the position is approximately **7.3 percentage points higher than the evaluation volatility of 22%, or 29.3%.**

iii. Increasing the dividend will lower the Month 2 forward price by approximately the amount of the increase, or 2.00. This is similar to lowering the stock price for Month 2. Since the total delta for Month 2 is –3,484, the effect on the total profit or loss will be approximately

$$-2.00 \times -34.84 = \textbf{69.68}$$

The increase in the dividend will increase the value of the position by approximately 69.68.

About the Author

Sheldon Natenberg has been working in options for more than three decades, initially as an independent floor trader at the Chicago Board Options Exchange and the Chicago Board of Trade, and later as an educator. In the latter role he has conducted seminars for option traders at major exchanges and professional trading firms in the United States, Europe, and the Far East.

Notes

Notes

Notes

Notes

Notes

Notes